Foundations of Intensional Semantics

Foundations of Intensional Semantics

Chris Fox and
Shalom Lappin

Blackwell
Publishing

BLACKWELL PUBLISHING
350 Main Street, Malden, MA 02148-5020, USA
9600 Garsington Road, Oxford OX4 2DQ, UK
550 Swanston Street, Carlton, Victoria 3053, Australia

First published 2005 by Blackwell Publishing Ltd

1 2005

Library of Congress Cataloging-in-Publication Data

Fox, Chris, 1965-
Foundations of intensional semantics / Chris Fox and Shalom Lappin.
p. cm.
Includes bibliographical references and index.
ISBN-13: 978-0-631-23375-6 (hardcover : alk. paper)
ISBN-10: 0-631-23375-X (hardcover : alk. paper)
ISBN-13: 978-0-631-23376-3 (pbk. : alk. paper)
ISBN-10: 0-631-23376-8 (pbk. : alk. paper)
1. Semantics. 2. Semantics (Philosophy) 3. Intension (Logic) 4. Semantics–Data processing. I. Lappin, Shalom. II. Title

P325.F657 2005
401′.43–dc22 2005010277

A catalogue record for this title is available from the British Library.

Set in Palatino 11/13.5
by SPI Publisher Services, Pondicherry, India
Printed and bound in the United Kingdom
by TJ International Ltd, Padstow, Cornwall

The publisher's policy is to use permanent paper from mills that operate a sustainable forestry policy, and which has been manufactured from pulp processed using acid-free and elementary chlorine-free practices. Furthermore, the publisher ensures that the text paper and cover board used have met acceptable environmental accreditation standards.

For further information on
Blackwell Publishing, visit our website:
www.blackwellpublishing.com

For my parents

לזכר אבי בן לפין המאיר את חיי

Contents

Preface

We began working on this book in 2000 in order to address several issues in the foundations of intensional logic and computational semantics that we felt had been neglected for too long in the these fields. Both of us had been thinking along parallel lines within different formal frameworks, and we wanted to explore the possibility of combining our respective approaches into a unified theory. In the course of writing the book, our ideas evolved considerably under pressure of joint research and helpful critical responses from colleagues. What we had originally envisaged as a one- or two-year project turned into a four-and-a-half-year odyssey through some of the most complex and recalcitrant problems in type theory and intensional semantics of natural language. We discovered that these problems are far more difficult than we had originally appreciated, and we came to understand why much of the field preferred to set them aside in favour of more tractable and empirically accessible questions.

We cannot claim that this book provides definitive solutions to the foundational questions that we set out to deal with, and, in many ways, the proposals that we present in this monograph represent work in progress. However, we do think that the theory of intensional semantics that we develop in this study offers a promising framework for a computationally viable semantic representation language, and we hope that this study will stimulate further work on the issues that we take up. Above all, we have learned a great deal about the nature of the problems that we address and the range of possible solutions to them. Our joint work has significantly enriched our understanding of the role of foundational issues in the development of an adequate semantic theory.

Earlier versions of the ideas discussed in this book were presented at Logical Aspects of Computational Linguistics 2001, (Le Crosic), Sinn und Bedeutung 2001 (Osnabrück), Seventh International Workshop on Natural Language Understanding and Logic Programming 2002 (Copenhagen), Seventh Symposium for Logic and Language 2002 (Pécs), Représentation du Sens 2003 (Montreal), Fields Workshop on Mathematical Linguistics 2003 (Ottawa), Logical Foundations of Computational Linguistics Workshop at Logic in Computer Science 2003 (Ottawa), Recent Advances in Natural Language Processing 2003 (Borovets), the Workshop on Lambda Calculus, Type Theory, and Natural Language (King's College, London) 2003, the Cognitive Science Colloquium, University of Osnabrück 2004, the Artificial Intelligence Colloquium of the Computer Science Department, Harvard University 2004, the Human Communication Research Centre Colloquium of the University of Edinburgh 2004, Strategies of Quantification 2004 (York), and the Eighth Symposium on Logic and Language 2004 (Debrecen). We are grateful to the participants of these forums for helpful discussion.

We would also like to thank Peter Aczel, Danny Bobrow, Robin Cooper, Cleo Condoravdi, Dick Crouch, Jan van Eijck, Nissim Francez, Dov Gabbay, Paul Gilmore, Jonathan Ginzburg, Howard Gregory, Ron Kaplan, Lauri Karttunen, Graham Katz, Ed Keenan, Kai-Uwe Kühnberger, Michael Kolhase, Jim Lambek, Peter Lasersohn, Tom Maibaum, Valeria Paiva, Gerald Penn, Ian Pratt-Hartmann, Steve Pulman, Michael Rabin, Dana Scott, Phil Scott, Kenneth Shan, Stuart Shieber, Mark Steedman, and Yoad Winter for helpful advice on a number of significant formal issues.

The second author used an earlier draft of this monograph as the main text of his MSc course in Advanced Computational Semantics for the Spring Semester of 2004, in the Department of Computer Science at King's College, London. The students in this course identified numerous mistakes in the book, and they offered many helpful suggestions for improving it. We are particularly indebted to Robert Schubert for careful, detailed and constructive comments on our proposed proof and model theories, and Christian Ebert, for his meticulous proof-reading and helpful feedback. We would also like to thank Adam Wyner for useful ideas on how to structure the book and for indicating ways in which we could render our formal concerns more accessible.

The chapter on a fine-grained higher-order intensional logic developed out of joint work with Carl Pollard. He has played an important role in shaping our ideas on general issues of intensionality and type theory, and we would like to thank him for his contribution to our work. We are also indebted to Ray Turner for reviewing the technical details presented in Chapters on Property Theory with Curry Typing, and for giving us insights into the issues of formal power and consistency. Needless to say, we bear sole responsibility for any errors that may remain in the book.

Finally, we owe a debt of gratitude to our respective families. Our wives and children have shown good-natured patience in the face of frequent joint working days in our homes, extended telephone calls at all hours of the day and night, ongoing email exchanges, and conference absences. They have even had to suffer our occasional jam sessions on guitar during breaks from our work. We have reluctantly accepted their urgent plea to put the band on hold and keep our day jobs. It seems that The Good Intensions will not be producing a hit record any time soon, but we do hope to implement components of our system in the near future.

The research of the second author has been supported by grant number AN/2687/APN from the Arts and Humanities Research Board of the UK, and grant number RES–000–23–0065 from the Economic and Social Research Council of the UK.

Chris Fox and Shalom Lappin
Wivenhoe and London

List of Abbreviations

ACE	antecedent contained ellipsis
BNF	Backus–Naur Form
CCC	Closed Cartesian Category
CG	Categorial Grammar
DRT	Discourse Representation Theory
FIL	Fine-grained Intensional Logic
GQ	Generalized Quantifier
HOU	higher-order unification
HPSG	Head-Driven Phrase Structure Grammar
IHOL	intensional higher-order logic
IL	intensional logic
ILF	interpreted logical form
ITT	intensional theory of types
LF	Logical Form
MLTT	Martin-Löf Type Theory
MS	Montague Semantics
NP	noun phrase
PLU	Logic Unplugged
PT	Property Theory
PTCT	Property Theory with Curry Typing
STT	Simple Theory of Types
UF	ultra filter
UT	Universal Type
UTIL	Untyped Intensional Logic
VP	verb phrase

Chapter 1

Introduction

The past 30 years have seen a vast expansion of research in formal and computational semantics of natural language. Much of this work has consisted in applications, extensions, and revisions of Montague's (1974) model of intensional semantics. This model has provided a remarkably enduring and effective framework for developing analyses of complex properties of natural language interpretation. It remains one of the most rigorously specified, elegant theories of meaning yet formulated. However, it suffers from a number of formal and empirical limitations, and the recognition of these shortcomings has provoked fruitful investigations of alternative approaches to Montague Semantics (MS). In most cases, these alternatives have been developed to address a particular set of problems with MS. They generally focus only on those aspects of the theory that prevent it from accommodating the phenomena with which they are concerned, while bypassing a systematic re-evaluation of its general architecture and foundational assumptions.[1]

Two important post-MS approaches that have played a prominent role in shaping research in semantic theory during the past

[1] See Dowty et al. (1981) for a classic introduction to MS. See Lappin (2000b) and Lappin (2003) for discussion of the three post-MS approaches to semantic theory sketched here.

two decades are dynamic semantics (Chierchia 1995; Groenendijk and Stokhof 1990, 1991; Heim 1982; Kamp 1981; Kamp and Reyle 1993) and situation semantics (Barwise and Etchemendy 1990; Barwise and Perry 1983; Cooper 1996; Seligman and Moss 1997). Dynamic semantics is devoted to modelling evolving relations of anaphora that emerge in discourse, between pronouns and certain types of definite descriptions, and their noun phrase antecedents. MS specifies the interpretations of sentences statically and in isolation. Therefore, it cannot handle the dynamic intersentential anaphora of discourse. Dynamic semantic theories propose representation languages that capture anaphoric dependencies exhibited in discourse sequences such as *A student arrived, He entered the class*, and in the donkey sentence *Every man who owns a donkey beats it*, where these dependencies are beyond the expressive resources of MS.

Situation semantics is concerned with the fact that MS represents the meaning of an expression in terms of its denotation in a possible world. MS uses an entire world, corresponding to a fully specified set of elementary facts, as a parameter for characterizing meaning. This creates difficulties for adequate analyses of reference, definite descriptions, and quantified NPs. Situation semanticists argue that these problems can be overcome if one substitutes situations (partial worlds) for worlds as the primary parameter relative to which the denotation of a term and the truth-value of a proposition are determined. Situations are fragments of worlds, and they provide a device for formally representing the contribution of contextual parameters to interpretation. So, for example, a definite description like *the book* does not have a unique denotation in most possible worlds, and certainly not in the actual world. However, it can be used to refer uniquely in an appropriately specified situation. Similarly, *Every student handed in a good paper* is false in the actual world, but true for an intended situation.

A third important trend in post-MS semantics is the move to underspecified semantic representations which leave the relative scope relations of quantified NPs and other scope-defining expressions (quantificational adverbs and adjectives, and negation) undefined in the interpretation of a sentence (Blackburn and Bos 2005; Bos 1995; Copestake et al. 1997; Crouch and van Genabith 1999; Dalrymple et al. 1999; Reyle 1993). The sentence *Every student wrote three programs for two courses* allows six possible scope readings corresponding to the six possible distinct linear orderings of its three quantified NP arguments. MS adopts the principle of compositionality, which requires that the meaning of an expression *E* is a function of the meanings of its constituents and the syntactic structure of *E*. MS takes the relation between syntax and semantics to be a homomorphism that maps all the elements of a syntactic category to the same semantic type. This entails that a sentence with six possible scope readings is ambiguous between six syntactic structures, each of which yields a representation with a distinct ordering of quantifiers. This approach generates spurious syntactic ambiguities that are not independently motivated by syntactic factors. If a single underspecified representation is assigned to the sentence, then one syntactic structure is sufficient, and unmotivated ambiguities are avoided. The underspecified representation can be resolved in different ways in order to generate the six scope readings.

While each of these approaches has contributed significant insights into semantic phenomena that MS is not able to capture adequately, none of them offers a systematic alternative to the basic assumptions underlying MS's notion of intension and its relation to modality. Nor do any of these approaches examine and revise the type theory within which MS encodes its intensional logic. Instead they each construct a task-specific logic that is intended to solve their own particular range of problems.

In this monograph we depart from the strategy of local revision that has driven much of post-MS research, and instead focus on the major design choices of the MS framework. We pursue two main objectives. First, we are concerned to show that it is necessary to characterize intensions independently of modality and treat them as basic elements of one's model theory in order to avoid the unattractive consequences of MS's reduction of intensional identity to logical equivalence. These consequences continue to infect most post-MS theories. Second, we intend to demonstrate that by adopting a radically revised type theory, and incorporating much of the semantic metalanguage within the representation language, it is possible to achieve a semantic theory that surpasses MS in expressive resources while remaining first-order in formal power. Moreover, this theory yields straightforward treatments of dynamic anaphora, ellipsis, and underspecified scope relations. We do not take up the role of contextual parameters in interpretation, which is the primary interest of situation semantics, but we are hopeful that our theory can be extended to cover this issue.

1.1 Montague's Intensional Logic

To set the stage for our study it is useful to review Montague's Intensional Logic (IL) in order to highlight those foundational assumptions that we will be examining and revising.[2]

1.1.1 The Syntax of IL

The Types

(1) Basic Types
    (a) t (truth-values)
    (b) e (individual entities)

(2) Exponential Types
    If a, b are types, then $\langle a, b\rangle$ is a type.[3]

(3) Intensional Types
    If a is a type, then $\langle s, a\rangle$ is a type (the type of the intension of a).

The basic types t, e correspond to the sentences (denotations of propositions) and the individual constants (the denotations of

[2] The following summary of IL is based upon Dowty et al. (1981, Chapter 6).

[3] We retain Montague idiosyncratic notation for exponential (function space) types. In specifying the type systems for other theories in later chapters we will use the more standard A^B (and $A \rightarrow B$).

proper names), respectively, in IL. An exponential type $\langle a, b\rangle$ is the functional type whose elements are functions from a to b. The members of the intensional type $\langle s, a\rangle$ are functions from indices (possible worlds) to denotations of the type a.

The Set ME_a of Well-Formed Expressions of Type a

(4) (a) Every variable of type a is in ME_a.
(b) Every constant of type a is in ME_a.
(c) If $\alpha \in ME_a$ and u is a variable in ME_b, then $\lambda u\alpha \in ME_{\langle b,a\rangle}$.
(d) If $\alpha \in ME_{\langle a,b\rangle}$ and $\beta \in ME_a$, then $\alpha(\beta) \in ME_b$.
(e) If $\alpha, \beta \in ME_a$, then $\alpha = \beta \in ME_t$.
(f) If $\phi, \psi \in ME_t$, then so are
i. $\sim\phi$
ii. $\phi \vee \psi$
iii. $\phi \wedge \psi$
iv. $\phi \rightarrow \psi$
v. $\phi \leftrightarrow \psi$.
(g) If $\phi \in ME_t$ and u is a variable in ME_a, then $\forall u\phi$ and $\exists u\phi \in ME_t$.
(h) If $\phi \in ME_t$, then $\Box\phi \in ME_t$.
(i) If $\alpha \in ME_a$, then $^\wedge\alpha \in ME_{\langle s,a\rangle}$
(j) If $\alpha \in ME_{\langle s,a\rangle}$, then $^\vee\alpha \in ME_a$

1.1.2 The Semantics of IL

A model $M = \langle A, W, F\rangle$ for IL is an ordered triple such that A and W are non empty sets (of entities and possible worlds, respectively), and for each type a of IL, F is a function from the non-logical constants of ME_a to interpretations of these constants. For each constant $c \in ME_a$ $F(c)$ is a function $f_c : W \rightarrow D_a$, where D_a is the domain of possible denotations for expressions of type a.[4]

[4] For simplicity we have omitted the ordered set of temporal points from M and the temporal operators F (future) and P (past) from this summary of IL.

The Set of Domains of Type a

Each non-logical constant of type a has a domain of possible denotations D_a. The set of these domains is defined recursively as follows:

(5) (a) $D_e = A$
(b) $D_t = 0, 1$
(c) $D_{\langle a,b \rangle} = {D_b}^{D_a}$
(d) $D_{\langle s,a \rangle} = {D_a}^W$

The Semantic Rules of IL

Let g be an assignment function such that for any variable $x \in a$ of IL, $g(x) \in D_a$, and for a model M of IL, assume $w \in W$. The expression $[\![\alpha]\!]_{M,w,g}$ denotes the evaluation of α in a model M, relative to a world w and an assignment function g. The following rules define the function $[\![\cdot]\!]_{M,w,g}$:

(6) (a) If α is a non-logical constant, then $[\![\alpha]\!]_{M,w,g} = (F(\alpha))(w)$.
(b) If α is a variable, then $[\![\alpha]\!]_{M,w,g} = g(\alpha)$.
(c) If $\alpha \in ME_a$ and u is a variable of type b, then $[\![\lambda u.\alpha]\!]_{M,w,g} = h : D_b \rightarrow D_a$ such that for any $d \in D_b$, $h(d) = [\![\alpha]\!]_{M,w,g[d/u]}$.
(d) If $\alpha, \beta \in ME_a$, then $[\![\alpha = \beta]\!]_{M,w,g} = 1$ iff $[\![\alpha]\!]_{M,w,g} = [\![\beta]\!]_{M,w,g}$.
(e) If $\phi \in ME_t$, then $[\![\sim \phi]\!]_{M,w,g} = 1$ iff $[\![\phi]\!]_{M,w,g} = 0$.
(f) If $\phi, \psi \in ME_t$, then $[\![\phi \vee \psi]\!]_{M,w,g} = 1$ iff $[\![\phi]\!]_{M,w,g} = 1$, or $[\![\psi]\!]_{M,w,g} = 1$.
(g) If $\phi, \psi \in ME_t$, then $[\![\phi \wedge \psi]\!]_{M,w,g} = 1$ iff $[\![\phi]\!]_{M,w,g} = 1$, and $[\![\psi]\!]_{M,w,g} = 1$.
(h) If $\phi, \psi \in ME_t$, then $[\![\phi \rightarrow \psi]\!]_{M,w,g} = 1$ iff $[\![\phi]\!]_{M,w,g} = 0$, or $[\![\psi]\!]_{M,w,g} = 1$.
(i) If $\phi, \psi \in ME_t$, then $[\![\phi \leftrightarrow \psi]\!]_{M,w,g} = 1$ iff $[\![\phi]\!]_{M,w,g} = [\![\psi]\!]_{M,w,g}$.
(j) If $\phi \in ME_t$ and u is a variable of type b, then $[\![\forall u \phi]\!]_{M,w,g} = 1$ iff for all $d \in D_b$, $[\![\phi]\!]_{M,w,g[d/u]} = 1$.
(k) If $\phi \in ME_t$ and u is a variable of type b, then $[\![\exists u \phi]\!]_{M,w,g} = 1$ iff for some $d \in D_b$, $[\![\phi]\!]_{M,w,g[d/u]} = 1$.
(l) If $\phi \in ME_t$, then $[\![\Box \phi]\!]_{M,w,g} = 1$ iff for all $w' \in W$, $[\![\phi]\!]_{M,w',g} = 1$.

(m) If $\alpha \in ME_a$, then $[\![^\wedge\alpha]\!]_{M,w,g} = h : W \rightarrow D_a$ such that for every $w' \in W, h(w') = [\![\alpha]\!]_{M,w',g}$.
(n) If $\alpha \in ME_{\langle s,a \rangle}$, then $[\![^\vee\alpha]\!]_{M,w,g} = ([\![\alpha]\!]_{M,w,g})(w)$.

Truth and Validity in IL
(7) If $\phi \in ME_t$, then $[\![\phi]\!]_{M,w} = t$ iff $[\![\phi]\!]_{M,w,g} = t$ for all g.

(8) If $\phi \in ME_t$, then ϕ is valid in IL iff $[\![\phi]\!]_{M,w} = t$ for all M and w.

1.2 Architectural Features of IL

We note three major architectural features of IL which we will examine and ultimately discard. First, following Carnap (1947), Montague defines intensions as functions from possible worlds to extensions. This definition is encoded in the semantic rule (6a), which specifies that the denotation of a non-logical constant α of IL in a model M, relative to a world w is the value at w of the intensional function that $F \in M$ assigns to α. IL contains an intensional operator $^\wedge$ that lifts an expression α to a term denoting α's intension (6m), and an extensional operator that lowers a term denoting an intension to one that denotes the corresponding extension (6n). Second, IL is a typed λ-calculus based on Church's (1940) Simple Theory of Types (STT) and supplemented by intensional types $\langle s, a \rangle$ for each a.[5] Third, IL is a higher-order logic with quantifiers and variables at each type in the hierarchy.

Each of these features gives rise to serious problems. Montague's characterization of intensions reduces intensional identity to equivalence of denotation across possible worlds. This view is unable to provide a sufficiently fine-grained treatment of meaning. It entails that logically equivalent expressions are co-intensional, and thus semantically indistinguishable. It requires that logically equivalent expressions be intersubstitutable in all contexts, including the complements of propositional attitude predicates. However, such substitutions do not always hold. So,

[5] Gallin (1975) simplifies Montague's type system by eliminating intensional types of this form and explicitly introducing a type corresponding to possible worlds.

for example, the sentences in (9) are logically equivalent, but the non-equivalence of the sentences in (10) shows that those in (9) are not co-intensional.

(9) (a) Every prime number is divisible only by itself and 1.
$\leftrightarrow$
(b) If $A \subseteq B$ and $B \subseteq A$, then $A = B$.

(10) (a) John believes that every prime number is divisible only by itself and 1.
(b) John believes that if $A \subseteq B$ and $B \subseteq A$, then $A = B$.

Despite the fact that variants of this problem have been recognized since Frege (1892), it has never been adequately solved. Its persistence remains an embarrassment to semantic theory whose foundations it continues to threaten. Developing a reasonable solution to this problem is one of our primary concerns in this monograph.

By adopting Church's STT, Montague commits IL to an inflexible and relatively impoverished type system that is not ideally suited to natural language semantics. Verbs, coordinating expressions, and other function-denoting terms generally apply to arguments of distinct types, which indicates that polymorphism is pervasive in natural language. Attempting to capture this fact within IL has resulted in the addition of awkward type raising and type changing operations. Allowing polymorphic types avoids these ad hoc devices. Also, IL requires that all non-basic types are exponential. Therefore, functions that apply to multiple arguments must be Curried, and this assumption implies, without independent motivation, that syntactic structure is binary. If product types are added, then functions can take several arguments simultaneously. Separation and comprehension types can be used to express semantic subtype relations, but these are not expressible in IL's version of the STT.

Finally, IL has significant expressive power by virtue of being higher-order. But there is a price to pay for this power. In general, the set of theorems of a higher-order logic is not recursively enumerable, and so its proof theory is incomplete. Clearly an enriched first-order theory that had sufficient expressive power to capture the main semantic properties of natural languages but remained complete would be a more attractive option.

Our general strategy is to first develop a formally adequate fine-grained account of intensions within a higher-order logic that is a conservative revision of IL and which preserves its type system. This permits us to concentrate on the problem of fine-grained intensionality in isolation from the others. We then adapt central elements of this account to a first-order property theory enriched with Curry typing (PTCT). In this theory we specify a type system that is flexible and rich enough to permit us to achieve expressive power comparable to a higher-order system like IL while remaining within the formal limits of a first-order system. It also allows for polymorphism and a range of non-exponential types.

We have abstracted away from questions concerning the interface between semantic representation and syntactic structure, and factored out the properties of the semantic representation language as our object of concern. The same procedures for computing the semantic representations of phrases and sentences on the basis of their syntactic structures that apply in Montague grammar or in alternative models of formal/computational theories of grammar can be assumed for the semantic representation languages that we develop here.

We describe PTCT as a first-order system. By this, we mean something stronger than just the fact that it has a first-order syntax. This issue is taken up in Section 9.5.

1.3 Structure of the Book

In Chapter 2 we review and compare several of the main proposals that have been advanced in post-MS work for a fine-grained theory of meaning. In order to render this comparison as transparent and precise as possible, we provide an algebraic reformulation of MS and consider the alternatives against this model. This approach permits us to identify two main options for a fine-grained theory of intensionality. One option is to extend the set of possible worlds (or situations) to include worlds (situations) which do not satisfy the meaning postulates that regulate the interpretation of non-logical constants of the representation language. This is an "impossible worlds" strategy for achieving fine-grained intensionality. It retains the MS view of intensions as functions from worlds (situations) to denotations. It gives rise to an unintuitive and problematic notion of interpretation. It also seems to require that the theory of meaning is dependent upon a theory of belief, which compromises the independence of semantics. The second option involves introducing distinct equality predicates for intensional identity and extensional equivalence in the representation language, and specifying the relation between them in the proof theory of the logic. In order to prevent the reduction of intensional identity to provable equivalence, it is necessary to model the entailment relation of the logic by a non-anti-symmetric preorder relation in a prelattice that models the proof theory. After considering both approaches in detail we adopt the second.

Chapter 3 introduces a simple, untyped, intensional theory (UTIL). This theory illustrates the basic approach that we develop to intensionality, particularly in the latter parts of the book. We discuss some of the theoretical issues that need to be addressed, both within the representation language, and within its domain of application. We then move to a basic version of Property Theory (PT) as an extension of UTIL. Our discussion of PT introduces some of the main ideas that we use in developing the enriched property theory of Chapter 5.

In Chapter 4 we specify a higher-order Fine-Grained Intensional Logic (FIL) in which the axioms of extensionality are replaced by weaker conditions on the relation between identity and equivalence. This is a conservative revision of Montague's semantics in which we seek to provide a more fine-grained notion of intensionality, while sustaining the basic type theory of IL. We introduce an equivalence (weak identity) predicate that can hold between any two expressions of the same type in addition to an intensional (strong) identity predicate. This chapter also gives an algebraic reduction of possible worlds (situations, indices) to prime filters in a prelattice of propositions. The algebraic semantics for FIL is the result of joint work with Carl Pollard.[6] While FIL succeeds in formalizing a fine-grained intensional logic in which intensionality is independent of modality, it retains the difficulties associated with MS's type theory and its higher-order formal power.

In Chapter 5 we show how our approach to fine-grained intensionality can be implemented in a first-order property theory. Large components of the semantic metalanguage of the theory are absorbed into the object language as the elements of a term sublanguage built with the untyped λ-calculus. This sublanguage enables us to represent propositions and other intensional entities as terms. We adopt Curry-style typing, which is more appropriate for natural language semantics than the rigid Church-style typing of IL and FIL. In particular, the system is extended to include separation, comprehension, product, and (weak) polymorphic types. In Property Theory with Curry Typing (PTCT) types are also terms of the language, and we impose constraints on both the type membership relation and the truth predicate to prevent the generation of semantic paradoxes. We define a tableau proof theory and a model theory for PTCT, and we prove soundness and completeness. We adopt this theory as our proposed semantic representation language. We illustrate its expressive power in subsequent chapters by using its type system to formulate a unified dynamic account of anaphora and ellipsis, and to construct a theory of underspecified representations.[7]

Chapter 6 adds an intensional number theory to both FIL and PTCT. This permits us to specify interpretations for generalized quantifiers (GQs) as relations between the cardinalities of properties, and, in the case of PTCT, of separation types. As a result, both theories can express higher-order GQs like *most*. In the case of PTCT, such GQs are encoded as terms in a first-order language. By incorporating a number theory based upon Peano axioms into PTCT, we render it incomplete. We consider using

[6] Needless to say, we bear sole responsibility for any mistakes that appear here. Earlier versions of FIL are presented in Fox and Lappin (2001) and Fox et al. (2002b).

[7] We presented earlier versions of PTCT in Fox and Lappin (2001), Fox et al. (2002a), and Fox et al. (2002c).

weaker number theories, such as Presburger arithmetic, in order to avoid this result and sustain the completeness of PTCT.

In Chapter 7 we apply the type system of PTCT to develop a dynamic unified account of anaphora and ellipsis. Operating at the interface between syntax and semantics, this presentation exploits the expressiveness of separation types within PTCT while maintaining a clear distinction between semantic and pragmatic issues.

In Chapter 8, we present a term-based theory of underspecification. In contrast to other approaches, we generate underspecified representations as λ-terms in the object language. This gives us access to the full expressive resources of PTCT in stating constraints on possible scope readings, and so we avoid the need to formulate a metalanguage for generating underspecified interpretations and restricting them. We use PTCT terms for underspecified scope representations as premises in inferences to (possibly fully) resolved conclusions. On our treatment of underspecified representations the proof theory that we specify for PTCT in Chapter 5 supports valid inferences of this kind without additional rules.

Chapter 9 takes up the issues of logical power and formal expressiveness in the context of computational semantics. One of the main advantages that we claim for PTCT is that it provides us with the rich resources of a higher-order system within a first-order system. This opens the way to implementing a computationally more tractable interpretation system without giving up the expressive capacity required to handle the semantic properties of natural language. In this chapter we also discuss what we mean by a "first-order system", and present evidence that PTCT's expressive and formal power is genuinely weaker than that of higher-order logic.

Finally, in Chapter 10, we discuss the main results of this study and consider directions for future work.

Chapter 2

Alternative Approaches to Fine-Grained Intensionality

As we saw in Chapter 1, the Carnap–Montague strategy of characterizing intensions in terms of modality (functions from possible worlds to extensions) results in a coarse-grained view of meaning on which intensional identity reduces to logical equivalence. In this chapter we will consider several attempts to construct a semantic theory that avoids this reduction. This work represents some of the main trends in hyperintensional semantics that have emerged over the past 25 years.

2.1 An Algebraic Representation of Possible Worlds Semantics

Before embarking on a review of the hyperintensionalist literature we will summarize some basic results of lattice theory and reformulate possible worlds semantics in lattice-theoretic terms.

This reformulation will provide us with a clear formal basis for comparing and evaluating the theories we look at.[8]

2.1.1 Algebras, Lattices, and Boolean Algebras

An *algebra* $A = \langle S, O_1, \ldots, O_n \rangle$ is a set S with operations $O_1, \ldots, O_n$ where

(11) for every $O_i \in A, S$ is closed under O_i, and

(12) for ever $a, b \in S$ and every $O_i \in A$, if $a = a'$ and $b = b'$, then $aO_ib = a'O_ib'$.

A *lattice* is an algebra $L = \langle A, \wedge, \vee \rangle$ in which the two binary operations $\wedge$ (meet) and $\vee$ (join) satisfy the following conditions:

(13) Idempotent Law
$a \wedge a = a$
$a \vee a = a$

(14) Commutative Law
$a \wedge b = b \wedge a$
$a \vee b = b \vee a$

(15) Associative Law
$(a \wedge b) \wedge c = a \wedge (b \wedge c)$
$(a \vee b) \vee c = a \vee (b \vee c)$

(16) Absorption Law
$a \wedge (a \vee b) = a$
$a \vee (a \wedge b) = a$

Definition 1 (Partially Ordered Set) *Let a* partially ordered set *(poset) be a set with an ordering relation $\leq$ on its elements.*

Definition 2 (Upper and Lower Bounds) *For a (poset) A,*
(1) a is an upper bound *of $B \subseteq A$ iff for all $b \in B, b \leq a$.*

[8] See Partee et al. (1990) for a discussion of algebras and lattices in formal linguistics.

(2) *a is the* least upper bound *of B iff for every upper bound c of B, $a \leq c$. The least upper bound of B is also known as the* supremum *of B* (sup *B*).
(3) *For a poset A, a is a* lower bound *of $B \subseteq A$ iff for every $b \in B$, $a \leq b$.*
(4) *a is the* greatest lower bound *of B iff for every lower bound c of B, $c \leq a$. The greatest lower bound of B is also known as the* infimum *of B* (inf *B*).

If a poset has a least upper bound and a greatest lower bound, they are unique by virtue of the antisymmetry of the partial order relation $\leq$.

Definition 3 (Alternative Definition of a Lattice) *It is possible to define a lattice $L = \langle A, \leq \rangle$ equivalently as a set A which is partially ordered by the relation $\leq$ such that $\leq$ is*
(1) *reflexive ($a \leq a$),*
(2) *antisymmetric (if $a \leq b$ and $b \leq a$, then $a = b$), and,*
(3) *transitive (if $a \leq b$ and $b \leq c$, then $a \leq c$), and further,*
(4) *for any $a, b \in A$, there exists* $\sup\{a,b\}$ *and* $\inf\{a,b\}$ *such that $a \wedge b = \inf\{a,b\}$, and $a \vee b = \sup a, b$.*

A *distributive lattice* is a lattice which satisfies the conditions of distributivity.

(17) Distributive Law

$$a \wedge (b \vee c) = (a \wedge b) \vee (a \wedge c)$$
$$a \vee (b \wedge c) = (a \vee b) \wedge (a \vee c)$$

A bounded lattice $L = \langle A, \wedge, \vee, 1, 0 \rangle$ is a lattice with a top element 1 (or $\top$), which is the least upper bound of A, and bottom element 0 (or $\bot$), which is the greatest lower bound of A.

An example of a bounded distributive lattice is the power set $\mathcal{P}(S)$ of a set S. $\mathcal{P}(S)$ is a bounded lattice in which A = the set of all subsets of S, $\wedge$ = set intersection, $\vee$ = set union, 1 = the union of all elements of $\mathcal{P}(S)$ (i.e. S), 0 = the empty set, and the partial ordering relation on $S = \subseteq$.

Definition 4 (Boolean Algebra) *A Boolean algebra is a bounded distributive lattice $L = \langle A, \wedge, \vee, \neg, 1, 0 \rangle$ with the unary operation $\neg : A \to A$ such that*

(1) for every $a \in A$, $\neg a$ = the complement of a,
(2) there is a partial order $\leq$ on A, 1 is $\top$ and 0 is $\bot$, and
(3) the distributive laws hold for the elements of A (that is, $a \wedge (b \vee c) = (a \wedge b) \vee (a \wedge c)$ and $a \vee (b \wedge c) = (a \vee b) \wedge (a \vee c)$).

In a Boolean algebra the following condition applies:

(18) $\neg\neg a = a$

(19) follows from (18) by virtue of the fact that (20) and (21) hold in a Boolean algebra.

(19) $a \vee \neg a = 1$

(20) $\neg(a \wedge \neg a) = 1$

(21) $\neg(a \wedge \neg a) = \neg a \vee \neg\neg a = \neg\neg a \vee \neg a = a \vee \neg a$

A Boolean algebra in which $A = \{1, 0\}$ is referred to as 2.

Classical propositional logic is modelled as a Boolean algebra in which the partial order relation on the set of propositions A of the lattice corresponds to entailment ($\vdash$).

2.1.2 Heyting Algebras

A Heyting algebra is a bounded distributive lattice $L = \langle A, \wedge, \rightarrow, \neg, 1, 0\rangle$ where $\rightarrow$ is a binary operation on A that for any $a, b \in A$, yields $a \rightarrow b$, the pseudo-complement of a relative to b. $a \rightarrow b$ is the largest element c in A such that $a \wedge c \leq b$. In a Heyting algebra the negation of a is defined as its pseudo-complement, i.e. $\neg a = a \rightarrow 0$. A Heyting algebra satisfies the following conditions:

(22) $a \rightarrow a = 1$

(23) $a \wedge (a \rightarrow b) = a \wedge b$

(24) $b \wedge (a \rightarrow b) = b$

(25) $a \rightarrow (b \wedge c) = (a \rightarrow b) \wedge (a \rightarrow c)$

However, (18) and (19) do not hold.

Heyting algebras model certain intuitionistic propositional logics. A Boolean algebra is a Heyting algebra that contains the complement operation, and so it satisfies (18) and (19).

2.1.3 Filters and Ideals

A subset I of a lattice L is an *ideal* if it satisfies (26)–(28):

(26) $0 \in I$

(27) If $a, b \in I$, then $a \vee b \in I$.

(28) If $a \in I$ and $b \leq a$, then $b \in I$.

A subset F of a lattice L is a *filter* if it satisfies (29)–(31):

(29) $1 \in F$

(30) If $a, b \in F$, then $a \wedge b \in F$.

(31) If $a \in F$ and $a \leq b$, then $b \in F$.

Filters and ideals are duals of each other.

The *principal ideal* generated by $a \in A$ is the subset $\downarrow (a) = \{b \in A : b \leq a\}$. $\downarrow (a)$ is the smallest ideal containing a.

The *principal filter* generated by $a \in A$ is the subset $\uparrow (a) = \{b \in A : a \leq b\}$. $\uparrow (a)$ is the smallest filter containing a.

A *prime ideal* PI is an ideal that satisfies (32) and (33):

(32) $1 \notin PI$

(33) If $a \wedge b \in PI$, then either $a \in PI$ or $b \in PI$.

A *prime filter* PF is a filter that satisfies (34) and (35):

(34) $0 \notin FI$

(35) If $a \vee b \in FI$, then either $a \in FI$ or $b \in FI$.

The complement of a prime ideal (prime filter) is a prime filter (prime ideal).

An *ultra filter UF* (*ultra ideal UI*) is a prime filter (prime ideal) which is maximal, i.e. it is not the case that there is a prime filter *PF′* (prime ideal *PI′*) such that $UF \subset PF'$ ($UI \subset PI'$).

2.1.4 Homomorphisms

A homomorphism $h : A \to B$ is a functional mapping between two algebras A and B which sustains the structure of A in B. Let A and B be algebras. If $0_i \; \varepsilon \; A$ corresponds to $0_i{}' \; \varepsilon \; B$, then for every $a, b \; \varepsilon \; A$, $h(a \; 0_i b) = h(a) \; 0_i{}' \; h(b)$. A homomorphism need not be one-to-one, but it preserves the algebraic structure and, in particular, the partial order of A in B. Consider the following theorem discussed in Bell (1999):

Theorem 1 *(i) I is a* prime ideal *of a Boolean algebra B iff there is a homomorphism* $h : B \to 2$ *such that* $I = h^{-1}(0)$ $(I = \{a : h(a) = 0\})$*; (ii) F is a* prime filter *of a Boolean algebra B iff there is a homomorphism* $h : B \to 2$ *such that* $F = h^{-1}(1)$ $(F = \{a : h(a) = 1\})$.

Theorem 1 establishes a one-to-one correspondence between the set of prime filters (prime ideals) of a Boolean algebra B and the set of homomorphisms $h : B \to 2$. For each prime filter PF (prime ideal PI) in B there is a homomorphism $h : B \to 2$ such that $h(a) = 1$ iff $a \; \varepsilon$ PF ($h(a) = 0$ iff $a \; \varepsilon$ PI). For each homomorphism $h : B \to 2 \; h^{-1}(1)$ is a prime filter in $B(h^{-1}(0))$ is a prime ideal in B).

Now consider the following theorem from Johnstone (1982, p. 14) and its corollary.

Theorem 2 (Johnstone) *For any* a, b *in a distributive lattice L such that* $a \nleq b$*, there is a homomorphism* $h : L \to 2$ *in which* $h(a) = 1$ *and* $h(b) = 0$.

Corollary 1 *For any* a, b *in a distributive lattice L, if every homomorphism* $h : L \to 2$ *is such that* $h(a) = h(b)$*, then* $a = b$.

Proof: If every homomorphism $h : L \to 2$ is such that $h(a) = h(b)$, then by Theorem 2 it is not the case that either $a \nleq b$ or $b \nleq a$. Therefore, $a \leq b$ and $b \leq a$. It follows that $a = b$ by the antisymmetry of the $\leq$ relation. Corollary 1 follows. □

2.2 Two Strategies for Hyperintensionalism

Corollary 1 specifies a direct connection between provability and the identity relation between propositions in a lattice. It has the consequence that if the entailment relation among propositions can be modelled as a partial order in a distributive lattice, identity of propositions reduces to logical equivalence (mutual entailment). If we formulate a semantic theory in algebraic terms, we can use Corollary 1 as an important measure of its success in avoiding this reduction.

This result implies that there are only two basic strategies that can be used to sustain a distinction between logical equivalence and intensional identity. On the first, impossible worlds are added to the model theory to permit propositions that are equivalent across the set of possible worlds to receive different truth-values. These impossible worlds violate either the meaning postulates governing the interpretations of non-logical constants in the language or the interpretations of logical constants fixed for the set of possible worlds.

The second strategy involves weakening the partial order relation that models entailment to a non-antisymmetric preorder in which mutual entailment does not force identity. This turns the algebraic structure of the semantic theory into a bounded distributive prelattice in which equivalent propositions are distinguished.[9] As we shall see in our survey of hyperintensionalist theories, most previous accounts either fail to clarify the nature of the entailment relation that they assume among propositions, or they adopt a variant of the impossible worlds approach. The exceptions to this generalization are Bealer's (1982) intensional logic and Property Theory (Turner 1992). Neither are formulated in algebraic terms, but the entailment relation that each assumes characterizes a preorder in a prelattice of propositions. We adopt alternative versions of the second strategy in the two semantic theories that we prospose in Chapters 4 and 5.

[9] We are grateful to Howard Gregory for first pointing out to us the possibility of using prelattices with non-antisymmetric preorder relations to avoid the consequences of Corollary 1.

We will characterize the two strategies of hyperintensionalism more precisely.

2.2.1 Impossible Worlds

If we model all natural language expressions, including generalized quantifier terms (quantificational determiners and certain kinds of modifiers) and connectives (coordinating expressions like *and* and *or*, and negation terms, like *not*) by non-logical constants in a logic, then their intepretation will be specified by meaning postulates that, added to the rules of the logic, define a semantic theory. Assume that a meaning postulate *MP* requires two non-logical constants c_i and c_j to have the same denotation in all models. Then c_i and c_j are provably equivalent in the theory of which *MP* is a part. One way of allowing c_i and c_j to be necessarily equivalent in this way while avoiding the conclusion that they have the same intension is to add models to one's model theory in which these violate *MP* by receiving distinct denotations. These models are, in effect, impossible worlds to the extent that they do not respect the intended interpretations of the expressions of a language as specified by its semantic theory.

Let L be a bounded distributive lattice whose elements are a set of propositions. We can identify the set of partial possible worlds with the set of prime filters of L, and the set of possible worlds W with the set of ultra filters of L. By Theorem 1 each prime filter PF of L corresponds to a mapping from L to 2 in which the elements of 2 receive the value 1. The complement of PF is a prime ideal PI of L whose elements receive the value 0. The union of a prime filter PF of L and its PI complement = L.

Let P be the set of axioms of the logic one has adopted for the semantic theory of a natural language L and MP the set of meaning postulates that constrain the interpretation of the non-logical constants of L. Construct a lattice A of propositions such that for any $a, b \in A$, $a \leq b$ iff $a \vdash_{P \cup MP} b$ (a entails b relative to $P \cup MP$). Given the Corollary 1, $a = b$ iff for every prime filter PF in A, $a \in PF$ iff $b \in PF$. Therefore, if a and b have the same truth-value in all possible worlds, then $a = b$, and equivalence across possible worlds reduces to identity of proposition.

Assume that we (i) treat all natural language terms as non-logical constants, and (ii) construct A so that $a \leq b$ iff $a \vdash_P b$. This permits homomorphisms $h : A \rightarrow 2$ such that $h(a) \neq h(b)$ even when $a \vdash_{MP} b$. The prime filters corresponding to these homomorphisms define worlds that are impossible relative to MP.

An obvious objection to using impossible worlds to distinguish between co-intensional expressions is that the prime filters corresponding to such worlds are defined by assigning distinct truth-values arbitrarily to propositions that are mutually entailing on their intended interpretations. Therefore, the differences in evaluation through which they establish distinctions in meaning are *ad hoc* and without content.

Barwise (1997) suggests a possible response to this objection. He proposes treating worlds (situations) as possible relative to a specified state of information. As information is added, the set of possibilities is reduced. So, for example, Fermat's Last Theorem was possibly not true relative to the information available at a point in time prior to the construction of a proof for it. When the proposition was proven, this possibility was excluded. Given this information-based view of possibility, we can treat the impossible worlds (situations) generated through the violation of meaning postulates as those that are possible relative to incomplete semantic information. The range of possibilities increases in proportion to the reduction in the amount of semantic information encoded in the constraints in MP. This would seem to provide an appropriate way of modelling the source of failure of intersubstitutability for co-intensional sentences in the complements of verbs and adjectives of propositional attitude. In principle, speakers may have only partial semantic information relative to which such sentences are not mutually entailing.

The problem with adopting this view in the context of a semantic theory is that it renders knowledge of meaning entirely dependent upon extra-linguistic knowledge. While some semanticists and philosophers have argued for such a dependence (most notably Quine (1960)), it seems to us to yield unacceptable results. Specifically, it excludes the possibility that a speaker is aware of the fact that two expressions are logically equivalent but still regards them as distinct in meaning. So, for example, it seems reasonable to insist that Fermat's Last Theorem and the statement asserting the consistency of the Continuum Hypothesis are distinct in meaning even if they are both true in all possible worlds.[10]

It is desirable, then, to construct a hyperintensional theory in which we are not forced to resort to an epistemic grounding of possible worlds as partial information states in order to salvage intensional distinctions between othewise provably equivalent propositions.

2.2.2 Modelling Entailment with a Preorder

Let A be an algebra that models the entailment relation $a \vdash_{PUMP} b$ with a preorder, which, in contrast to a partial order, is not, in general, antisymmetric. The algebra is then a prelattice rather than a lattice. It models a logic in which the Axiom of Extensionality, given in (36), does not hold. Entailment is reflexive and transitive, but not antisymmetric.

(36) $a \leftrightarrow b \vdash a = b$

This approach requires an independent characterization of the identity predicate = in the logic on which it is possible for it to be the case that for every homomorphism $h : A \to 2$, $h(a) = h(b)$, but $a \neq b$. Characterizing entailment as a non-antisymmetric preorder permits one to treat a set of logically equivalent expressions as an equivalence class whose elements do not reduce

[10] Gregory (2002) proposes a relevance logic which uses a variant of an impossible worlds strategy. Logical truths do not hold in all worlds. Formulas are evaluated only relative to those worlds satisfying particular accessibility relations (the set of relevant situations), and different formulas may be considered relative to distinct worlds. Logically equivalent propositions can be distinguished if they are evaluated in different set of worlds. This approach to impossible worlds seems close in spirit to Barwise's view. The formal notion of relevance appears to encode an epistemically-based relation between possible worlds. It is not immediately clear how this system accommodates the possibility that a speaker recognizes two sentences as having the same truth-value in all and only the same situations but still identifies them as distinct in meaning.

to a single element, as they do for classes of terms in a full lattice for which the partial order relation holds in both directions. The two semantic theories that we present in Chapters 4 and 5, respectively, each contain two internal equality predicates. One corresponds to intensional identity and the other to extensional equivalence. In the logics that support these theories the identity of two expressions entails their equivalence, but the converse does not hold. Therefore, these theories can distinguish between provable equivalence and intensional identity without invoking impossible worlds or other modal (epistemic) devices.

2.3 Thomason's Intentional Logic

Thomason (1980) proposes a higher-order intensional logic, which he calls Intentional Logic (IL_T). In this logic, a type p of propositions is added to e (individuals) and t (truth-values) in the set of basic types. The classical truth functions, quantifiers, and the identity relation are defined as functions from types τ to t. A parallel set of intentional connectives, quantifiers, and an identity relation are defined as functions from types τ to p. An extensional operator $^{\cup}\langle p,t\rangle$ denotes a homomorphism from D_p to 2, the bounded distributive lattice containing only 1 and 0 (equivalently, $\top$ and $\bot$).

The basic elements of IL_T are as follows:

(37) (a) Basic types: e, t, p
(b) Derived types: If σ, τ are types, then $\langle \sigma, \tau\rangle$ is a type.
(c) Intentional Connectives
i. $\sim$ (of type $\langle p, p\rangle$)
ii. $\cap$ (of type $\langle p, \langle p, p\rangle\rangle$)
iii. $\cup$ (of type $\langle p, \langle p, p\rangle\rangle$)
iv. $\supset$ (of type $\langle p, \langle p, p\rangle\rangle$)
(d) Extensional Connectives
i. $\neg$ (of type $\langle t, t\rangle$)
ii. $\wedge$ (of type $\langle t, \langle t, t\rangle\rangle$)

iii. $\vee$ (of type $\langle t, \langle t, t\rangle\rangle$)
iv. $\sqsupset$ (of type $\langle t, \langle t, t\rangle\rangle$)

(e) Intentional Quantifiers
$\bigcap$ (of type $\langle\langle\tau, p\rangle, p\rangle$)

(f) Extensional Quantifiers
$\bigwedge$ (of type $\langle\langle\tau, t\rangle, t\rangle$)

(g) Intentional Identity
$\approx$ (of type $\langle\tau, \langle\tau, p\rangle\rangle$)

(h) Extensional Identity
$=$ (of type $\langle\tau, \langle\tau, t\rangle\rangle$)

(i) Extensional Operator
$^{\cup}$ (of type $\langle p, t\rangle$)

A model IL_T is specified by a function $Val : \alpha_\tau \rightarrow D_\tau$, where α_τ is an expression of IL_T in type τ and D_τ is the domain of values for expressions of this type, and the following conditions hold:

(38) (a) $Val(\alpha(\beta)) = Val(\alpha)(Val(\beta))$
(b) $Val(\lambda u^\sigma.\phi_\tau) =$ the function f in $D_{\langle\sigma,\tau\rangle}$, such that for any $a \in D_\sigma$, $f(a) = Val^{[a/u]}(\phi)$
(c) *Val* assigns the classical truth functions to the extensional connectives, the classical GQ functions to the extensional quantifiers, and the function $f : D_\tau \rightarrow (D_\tau \rightarrow D_t)$ to the extensional identity predicate such that $(f(=)(Val(a)))(Val(b)) = t$ iff $Val(a) = Val(b)$.
(d) $Val(^{\cup})$ is a function $h : D_p \rightarrow 2$ such that h is a homomorphism from D_p to 2.

The set of homomorphisms which can provide the interpretation of the extensional operator is constrained by meaning postulates such as the following:

(39) (a) $\bigwedge y^p(^{\cup}\sim y = \neg^{\cup}y)$
(b) $\bigwedge y^p z^p(^{\cup}(y \cup z) = {^{\cup}y} \wedge {^{\cup}z})$
(c) $^{\cup}\bigcap x^\tau\phi = \bigwedge x^{\tau\cup}\phi$
(d) $^{\cup}(\alpha \approx \beta) = (\alpha = \beta)$

(40) $\bigwedge x^e(^{\cup}groundhog'_{\langle e,p\rangle}(x) = {^{\cup}woodchuck'_{\langle e,p\rangle}}(x))$

This last axiom (40) requires that for any individual a, the truth-value of $^{\cup}groundhog'(a)$ is identical to that of $^{\cup}woodchuck'(a)$. It does not require that $groundhog'(a)$ and $woodchuck'(a)$ be identical propositions, and so it is compatible with (41).

(41) $\bigwedge x^{e}\neg(groundhog'(x) = woodchuck'(x))$

The main problem with Thomason's proposal is that he does not specify the algebraic structure of the domain of propositions D_p or the entailment relation which holds among its elements. The connection between intentional identity and intentional bi-implication is not specified, and so the interpretation of these relations is crucially underdetermined.

Given Corollary 1, if D_p is a bounded distributive lattice, then Thomason must allow the set of homomorphisms from D_p to 2 that provide possible intepretations of the extensional operator $^{\cup}\langle p, t\rangle$ to contain mappings from D_p to 2 which do not respect the meaning postulates that he imposes upon this operator. Such homomorphisms will specify impossible worlds that distinguish between non-identical propositions that the meaning postulates require to be identical in truth-value in the subset of homomorphisms corresponding to the intended interpretations of the elements of D_p.

Alternatively, Thomason could characterize D_p as a prelattice whose preorder is not antisymmetric. However, he does not provide a proof theory for IL_T that specifies an entailment relation for the elements of D_p, and these central issues remain unsettled. Therefore, it is not clear precisely how Thomason's Intentional Logic permits us to distinguish between logically equivalent expressions.

2.4 Bealer's Intensional Logic

Bealer (1982) proposes an intensional logic L_ω with the syntax of classical first-order logic supplemented by an abstraction operator $[A]_{v_1,\ldots,v_k}$. This operator forms a term denoting the intension of A and binding the free variables $v_1, \ldots, v_k$ in A. He provides an algebraic model theory for L_ω in which the domain D is partitioned into disjoint subsets $D_{0-1}, D_0, D_1, \ldots, D_k$ of individuals (D_{0-1}, a possibly empty set), propositions (D_0), properties (D_1), and k-ary relations in intension (D_k), respectively. Id, Conj, Neg, and Exist are algebraic operations that interpret the identity predicate and the Boolean logical constants of L_ω. A family of operations $Pred_i$ interpret complex terms formed by abstraction. K is a set of functions that assign extensions to the elements of D. In Bealer's system the expressions of L_ω denote intensions in D, and these are assigned extensions.

Bealer also provides two variants of an axiomatic proof theory for L_ω. The first contains a version of the axiom of extensionality, and so in this formulation of L_ω logical equivalence entails intensional identity. The second version dispenses with the axiom and permits distinct propositions to be provably equivalent. Bealer does not specify an ordering relation for D_0, the set of propositions, in his model theory. In order to sustain his second proof theory for L_ω it is necessary to supplement his algebraic semantics with the requirement that the entailment relation is modelled by a non-antisymmetric preorder on D_0 for the set of models that support it.

Bealer's intensional logic represents a radical departure from the classical view of intensionality developed in the work of Carnap and Montague. He treats intensions as primitive elements of a domain in a model rather than as functions from possible worlds or other indices to extensions. This approach permits him to characterize intensions independently of modality. He constructs a proof theory which specifies the relation between intensional identity and provable equivalence in a way that allows for fine-grained intensionality. However, it suffers from a number of serious formal difficulties.

First, Bealer's insistence on using a first-order logic without functional types restricts the expressive power of his system in a way that prevents it from representing central features of natural language semantics. His logic seems unable to express the full range of generalized quantifiers (functions from properties to propositions) or modifiers (functions from properties to properties, and functions from propositions to propositions). Therefore, it cannot model the interpretations of many determiners, verb phrase and sentential adverbs, and adjectives.

Second, Bealer's claim that he avoids functions as denotations for terms in his logic is problematic. He uses a $Pred_i$ operation to interpret a complex term generated by applying one abstraction term to another. So, for example, applying the property term $[Fx]_x$ to the relation term $[Guv]_{u,v}$ yields the propositional term $[F[Guv]_{u,v}]$ which denotes $Pred_0([Fx]_x, [Guv]_{u,v}])$.[11] Let $H \in K$ (H is a function from elements of D to extensions). In Bealer's model theory, $H([F[Guv]_{u,v}] = T$ iff $[Guv]_{u,v} \in H([Fx]_x)$. But this interpretation of $[F[Guv]_{u,v}]$ implies that $[Fx]_x$ denotes the characteristic function of a set. In fact, Bealer's abstraction operator looks very much like a lambda operator. It is difficult to see how one can avoid computing the denotations of abstraction terms by treating them as standing for the same kinds of functions that interpret lambda terms.

Finally, because the formation of abstraction terms is not governed by type constraints, it can generate semantic paradoxes analogous to those that arise in the untyped λ-calculus. Let M be a model and I an interpretation function. Assume that $I(F) \in D_1$ (a unary property), and for all $H \in K, H(F) = S \subseteq D_1$, where S is the set of unary properties such that for any unary predicate G, if $I(G) \in S$, then $H([G([Gx]_x]) = F$. Therefore, F denotes the property of being a property that does not apply to itself. It follows that $[F[Fx]_x]$ denotes a proposition that is true iff it is false.[12]

This paradox is not generated directly in L_ω but in the metalanguage used to describe its model theory. It could be blocked by imposing a syntactic condition on term abstraction that prevents self-application. Such a condition would, in effect, introduce type constraints into the logic. Alternatively, one could attempt to

[11] We are following Bealer here in using $[Fx]_x$ and $[Guv]_{u,v}$ to represent their denotations in $Pred_0([Fx]_x, [Guv]_{u,v}])$ and in other metalinguistic expressions that describe model theoretic entities.

[12] While Bealer suggests the analogue of set theoretic axioms to restrict a predication relation δ, added in a later chapter to his logic, in order to avoid semantic paradoxes, from what we can see, he does not limit the interpretation of the abstraction operator to rule out the paradox described here.

formulate restrictions on the set of propositions in D_0 that prevent terms formed through self-application of the sort that leads to paradox from denoting propositions. Both of these strategies are employed in Property Theory, which incorporates the untyped λ-calculus to construct a language of terms embedded within a first-order logic with a truth predicate. Turner (1992) applies the latter approach. He develops a Property Theory with a many-sorted domain in which predicates are used to filter the set of propositions and so prevent paradoxes. In Chapter 5 we adopt the former strategy in constructing a Property Theory that uses Curry typing of terms.

Despite its significant formal shortcomings, Bealer's logic presents an interesting and original attempt to construct a fine-grained intensional semantics in which the proof and model theories are designed to prevent the collapse of intensional identity into logical equivalence. We adopt certain aspects of his approach in developing both a higher-order fine-grained intensional logic in Chapter 4 and a first-order Property Theory with Curry typing in Chapter 5.

2.5 Structured Meanings and Interpreted Logical Forms

Cresswell (1985) proposes a notion of intension in which the syntactic structure of an expression plays a role in individuating its meaning. Cresswell interprets a *that* complementizer as a function from a sentential complement C to the sequence of intensions associated with the syntactic constituents of C. Therefore, if we take $[\![Phil']\!]_M$ to be a generalized quantifier of type $\langle\langle s,\langle e,t\rangle\rangle,t\rangle$ and $[\![groundhog']\!]_M$ to be a property of type $\langle s,\langle e,t\rangle\rangle$, then the denotation of *that Phil is a groundhog*, the complement of *believes* in (42), is the sequence in (43).

(42) Mary believes that Phil is a groundhog.

(43) $\langle [\![Phil']\!]_M, [\![groundhog']\!]_M \rangle$

On Cresswell's account, a propositional attitude verb denotes a relation between individuals and propositions interpreted as structured meanings. Two propositions which have identical truth-values across possible worlds but correspond to different sequences of intensions are distinct and thus not intersubstitutable as objects of propositional attitude.

Cresswell's theory is a development of Carnap's (1947) notion of intensional isomorphism. Two expressions α, β are intensionally isomorphic iff they have the same syntactic structure at each point i in their respective syntactic constructions, and at each point i for α, the intension of the constituent at i has the same intension as the corresponding constituent at i for β. While Carnap defines intensional isomorphism only for first-order languages, Cresswell applies the concept of structured meanings to a higher-order language similar to Montague's IL.

Although structured meanings provide a more finely grained specification of meaning than intensional functions from indices to truth-values (propositions in IL), they do not distinguish between the complements of (42) and (44).

(44) Mary believes that Phil is a woodchuck

(45) $\langle [\![Phil']\!]_M, [\![woodchuck']\!]_M \rangle$

If we assume that for all M, $[\![groundhog']\!]_M = [\![woodchuck']\!]_M$, then the structured meanings in (43) and (45) are identical.

Larson and Segal (1995) (L&S) propose a variant of the structured meaning approach which avoids this problem. They suggest that the interpreted logical form (ILF) of a sentence is the interpreted syntactic tree that appears as the final (LF) element of its syntactic derivation. Each node of the ILF tree is a pair containing the name of the node (a constituent type or, at the terminal nodes, a lexical item) and its extension. While L&S characterize ILFs in terms of the extensions of the syntactic constituents in an ILF tree, it is possible to substitute intensions for the second elements of the ordered pairs at the nodes of the ILF tree. The lexical items in the NP *a groundhog* are distinct from those of the NP *a woodchuck*. Therefore, the ILF associated with the complement of

(42) is distinct from ILF for the complement of (44). Unlike structured meanings, ILFs include the lexical items at the terminal nodes of the syntactic tree that partially identifies the intension of an expression. Hence ILFs allow us to individuate meanings as finely as distinct expressions in a language.

In order to represent meaning containment and synonymy among expressions of a language it is necessary to establish entailments and relations of equivalence between ILFs. To model entailment for a set A of ILFs, it is necessary to define an algebraic structure with an ordering relation for the elements of A. These elements are evaluated by homomorphisms $h : A \rightarrow 2$. Once again the two options present themselves. (i) If the entailment relation for A is expressed by a partial order and A is a distributive lattice, then for any two ILFs $a, b \in A$ which are such that for all homomorphisms $h : A \rightarrow 2$, if $h(a) = h(b)$, then $a = b$. To distinguish between ILFs which are taken as identical in truth-value but different in meaning, it will be necessary to admit homomorphisms that assign them different truth-values. These mappings from A to 2 correspond to prime filters of A that specify impossible worlds. Alternatively, (ii) entailment is not represented by a partial order. But then we require an alternative characterization of entailment and identity for ILF. Specifically, we need a proof theory, and a theory of identity for ILF.

2.6 Landman's Data Semantics

Landman (1986a) suggests that logically equivalent propositions in a formal language can be distinguished if they are constructed from distinct elementary propositions. This idea is similar in spirit to Carnap's notion of intensional isomorphism.

Landman (1986a) uses a distributive De Morgan lattice to model a first-order language. A lattice of this type satisfies the De Morgan laws (46), (47) and double negation (18) (repeated here as (48)):

(46) $\neg(a \vee b) = \neg a \wedge \neg b$

(47) $\neg(a \wedge b) = \neg a \vee \neg b$

(48) $\neg\neg a = a$

On Landman's theory a model $M = \langle A, [\![\cdot]\!]\rangle$ for a first-order language L_0, is an ordered pair in which A is a distributive De Morgan lattice and $[\![\cdot]\!]$ is an interpretation function. An $a \in A$ is *founded on* $X \subseteq A$ iff for some $x_1, \ldots, x_n \in X, x_1 \wedge \ldots \wedge x_n \leq a$. The filter F_B generated by $B \subseteq A = \{a \in A : a \text{ is founded on } D\}$. A sentence ϕ in L_0 is true in M on the basis of $B \subseteq A$ iff $[\![\phi]\!]_M \in F_B$. A sentence ϕ in L_0 is false in M on the basis of $B \subseteq A$ iff $\neg[\![\phi]\!]_M \in F_B$.

Facts are elementary (non-negated) elements of A, and propositions are constructed out of facts by applying the operations of the lattice to facts. A proposition p is constructed out of the facts $f_1, \ldots, f_n$ if applying operations of A to $f_1, \ldots, f_n$ yields p. Let $p = a \vee \neg a$ and $q = b \vee \neg b$, where a, b are distinct facts in A. Landman claims that although p and q are mutually entailing in A, $p \neq q$ because they are constructed out of different facts.

It is not clear how Landman can sustain this distinction between logically true (false) propositions. The partial order that defines A is antisymmetric. If we assume that A is a bounded lattice of propositions, then both p and $q = \top$, and so $p = q$. Similarly, all logically false propositions are identical to $\bot$. If A is not bounded, then it cannot model a logic of the type Landman intends it to.

Assume that the set of possible models is restricted to models which respect the meaning postulates of the language. If p and q receive the same truth-value in all models, then they will entail each other in A. Therefore, they are identical by virtue of the antisymmetry of the partial order relation of A. Alternatively, the set of possible models contains elements that specify impossible worlds. It seems that given his decision to use a full partial order to model entailment, Landman has not escaped the need to postulate impossible worlds in order to avoid the intensional collapse of logically equivalent propositions.

2.7 Situation Semantics and Infon Algebras

Barwise and Perry (1983) propose a framework in which information (the content of a proposition) is evaluated against a situation, which is a part of a world, rather than a complete world. They refer to the informational content of a proposition as an *infon*, and they characterize a proposition as an assertion that a specified situation s *supports* an infon σ. Unlike possible worlds, situations are not disjoint but partially ordered by a containment relation. Situation semantics develops a more finely textured account of the relation between propositional content and entities in the world than Montague semantics does by virtue of the fact that it can connect the same informational content to distinct situations in a single world.

Barwise and Etchemendy (1990) propose an infon algebra as the framework for developing the model theory of situation semantics.

Definition 5 (Infon Algebra) *An infon algebra* $\mathcal{I} = \langle Sit, I, \Rightarrow, \models \rangle$ *where Sit is a non-empty set of situations, I is a non-empty set of infons,* $\langle I, \Rightarrow \rangle$ *is a bounded distributive lattice, and* $\models$ *is a relation on* $Sit \times I$ *that satisfies the following conditions, where* $s \in Sit$ *and* $\sigma, \tau \in I$.
(1) *If* $s \models \sigma$ *and* $\sigma \Rightarrow \tau$, *then* $s \models \tau$.
(2) $\neg(s \models 0)$ *and* $s \models 1$.
(3) *If* Σ *is a finite set of infons, then* $s \models \wedge\Sigma$ *iff for each* $\sigma \in \Sigma, s \models \sigma$.
(4) *If* Σ *is a finite set of infons, then* $s \models \vee\Sigma$ *iff for some* $\sigma \in \Sigma, s \models \sigma$.

The conditions that Definition 5 imposes on the $\models$ relation require that the set of infons which a situation supports is a prime filter.

$Supports : I \rightarrow \mathcal{P}(Sit)$ is a homomorphism from the set of infons to the power set of situations such that for each $\sigma \in I, Supports(\sigma) = \{s \in Sit : s \models \sigma\}$. Consider the following generalization of Johnstone's theorem (Theorem 2).

Theorem 3 (Generalized Johnstone) *Let L be a bounded distributive lattice. For any* a, b *in a distributive lattice A, if every homomorphism* $h : A \rightarrow L$ *is such that* $h(a) = h(b)$, *then* $a = b$.

Proof: It follows from Theorem 2 that for any a, b in a distributive lattice A such that $a \not\leq b$ there is a homomorphism $g : A \rightarrow 2$ in which $g(a) = 1$ and $g(b) = 0$. 2 can be embedded in any bounded distributive lattice L by the homomorphism $f : 2 \rightarrow L$ which is such that $f(1) = 1$ and $f(0) = 0$. Let $h : A \rightarrow L = f \circ g$. Then for any a, b in a distributive lattice A such that $a \not\leq b$, there is a homomorphism $h : A \rightarrow L$ in which $h(a) \neq h(b)$. The theorem follows. □

The power set of situations is a bounded distributive lattice. Therefore, if for all homomorphisms $h : I \rightarrow \mathcal{P}(Sit)$ that are permitted instances of *Supports*, two infons $\sigma, \tau \in I$ are such that $h(\sigma) = h(\tau)$, then $\sigma = \tau$. But then in order to distinguish between two infons σ and τ which are logically equivalent or equivalent by virtue of meaning postulates, it is necessary to posit homomorphisms from I to $\mathcal{P}(Sit)$ in which $h(\sigma) \neq h(\tau)$. These homomorphisms correspond to impossible situations (impossible partial worlds).

Assume that $\sigma = \langle\langle groundhog'; Phil', \alpha\rangle\rangle$ and $\tau = \langle\langle woodchuck'; Phil', \alpha\rangle\rangle$. σ represents the informational content that Phil is a groundhog, with α indicating a positive or negative judgement, and similarly for τ. If the set of homomorphisms H which can provide instances of *Supports* is constrained by meaning postulates of the form (49), then $\sigma = \tau$.

(49) For every $s \in Sit, s \models \sigma$ iff $s \models \tau$.

Alternatively, if H contains elements that violate the meaning postulates, then these mappings from I to $\mathcal{P}(Sit)$ characterize impossible situations (impossible partial worlds). Therefore, the version of situation theory presented in Barwise and Etchemendy (1990) does not avoid the need to invoke impossible worlds in order to avoid intensional collapse.

2.8 Situations as Partial Models

Muskens (1995) uses a many-valued logic to define indices as partial models rather than complete worlds. Indices correspond to situations, and, like situations, they are partially ordered by (distinct types of) containment relations. A partial model M is the indexed union of a set of indices, where each index in the set is an indexed partial model M_i corresponding to a situation i.

Let Γ, Δ be sets of propositions. Δ *strongly follows* from Γ iff in every intended model M (a model that satisfies a given set of axioms), the partial intersection of values of the elements of Γ is included in the partial union of the values of the elements of Δ. For two propositions p and q, q *weakly follows* from p iff for every intended model M, in each M_i of M that satisfies a specified set of meaning postulates, the value of p in M_i is (partially) included in the value of q at M_i.

Substitution of propositional arguments in predicates denoting relations of propositional attitude is restricted to cases of strong mutual entailment. (50a) and (50b) weakly entail each other.

(50) (a) $groundhog'(c)$
(b) $woodchuck'(c)$

They are equivalent only in the partial models that satisfy the meaning postulate in (51).

(51) $\lambda i[\forall x(groundhog'(x,i) = woodchuck'(x,i))]$

As (50a) and (50b) are weakly synonymous, they are not intersubstitutable in belief contexts.

Muskens' notion of weak entailment relies on the satisfaction of meaning postulates in a set of partial models. Strong entailment does not, in general, sustain the relations of extra-logical synonymy encoded in these postulates. Hence, his analysis of co-intensionality and intersubstitutivity in the complements of propositional attitude verbs appears to require impossible (partial) worlds to distinguish between synonymous propositions that are not logically equivalent. However, this analysis does not seem to avoid the intensional collapse of logically equivalent propositions, as these are strongly mutually entailing.

2.9 Topos Semantics

Lappin and Pollard (1999) (L&P) propose an intensional semantic theory based upon category theory. In this system, linguistic expressions of a natural language are interpreted by arrows (corresponding to functions) in a non-extensional topos. These objects serve as the intensions of natural language expressions. Possible worlds are defined algebraically as ultra filters of propositions in the lattice of propositions for a topos, a certain kind of closed Cartesian category. Extensions are derivative entities characterized in terms of membership in these ultra filters.

(52) *Categories* are labelled graphs whose edge labels, called *arrows*, satisfy the familiar laws of identity and composition that functions satisfy.

(53) A closed Cartesian category (CCC) is a category with sufficient structure to provide a model of a higher-order typed λ-calculus.

(54) A CCC contains
  (a) terminal objects (the categorical counterparts of singleton sets);
  (b) Cartesian products (corresponding to product types); and
  (c) exponentials (the counterpart of functional types).

(55) For any category with the terminal object 1, we can think of an arrow $f : 1 \to A$ as the categorical generalization of the set theoretic notion of a member of A. This arrow is a mapping from a terminal object 1, corresponding to a singleton set, to a subobject A, corresponding to a set.

(56) A *topos* is a CCC with a distinguished object Ω that corresponds to the type of propositions, and an arrow (called true) $1 \to \Omega$ that has the property of being a *subobject classifier*. In a topos a *predicate* is an arrow $r : A \to \Omega$.

(57) Using the subobject classifier, predicates can be viewed as categorical counterparts of characteristic functions of 'subsets' (actually subobjects) of A.

L&P take the linguistic topos **T** to be the *free* topos generated over a single basic type I (for individuals) and a set of basic arrows for word meanings. All other objects, specifically Ω, 0, 1, and objects obtained from these and I as products, co-products, exponentials, and subobjects, are generated directly by topos theory. Proper names, intransitive verbs, transitive verbs, and verbs of propositional attitude are arrows of the types $1 \to I$, $I \to \Omega$, $(I \otimes I) \to \Omega$, and $(I \otimes \Omega) \to \Omega$, respectively.

Following Lambek and Scott (1986), L&P employ the notion of the *internal language* $L(K)$ of a given CCC K, a higher-order typed λ-calculus for which equivalence classes of closed terms are in a natural one-to-one correspondence with arrows of K (specifically, with the arrows with domain 1). L&P use the internal language of the linguistic topos, $L(\mathbf{T})$, as a semantic representation language for natural language. An expression of $L(\mathbf{T})$ looks like a term in any familiar typed λ-calculus, such as Gallin's (1975) Ty2. However, these expressions denote not functions but arrows of T. In contrast to Montague semantics, in this framework there is a single fixed intended model in which the expressions of a language are interpreted. This model is the linguistic topos **T** whose arrows are construed as intensions.

Unfortunately, shortly after L&P proposed their topos semantics, Pollard recognized that it was fatally flawed. The propositions of a free topos form a Heyting algebra for which the axiom of extensionality holds. This axiom specifies that if two propositions are equivalent, then they are identical, Therefore, for any prime filter PF of propositions of **T**, if $a, b \in PF$, then $a = b$ in PF. This form of intensional collapse is considerably more acute than the reduction of co-intensionality to logical equivalence. It entails that all propositions that are true in a given world are indistinguishable in that world.

In recent work Pollard (2004) has given an outline of an alternative category-theoretic semantics that avoids this problem. He identifies the class of propositions in his CCC with an object distinct from Ω and takes the ordering relation of the algebra of propositions that this CCC generates to be a non-antisymmetric preorder. The higher-order typed λ-calculus that corresponds to the CCC bears certain similarities to the higher-order system FIL, which we propose in Chapter 4, but its type system is richer and more articulated along the lines of the types that we develop for our first-order Property Theory with Curry Typing in Chapter 5.

2.10 Conclusion

We have used an algebraic paradigm of semantic theory to clarify the possibilities for a viable hyperintensionalist semantics. Examination of this paradigm suggests that there are two basic strategies that can be pursued in order to sustain intensional distinctions among provably equivalent expressions.

One is to add impossible worlds to one's model theory, where these worlds violate some of the meaning postulates governing the interpretation of constants (logical and non-logical) in one's language. Aside from the apparent inelegance of this device, accommodating impossible worlds requires rendering semantic theory dependent on a theory of belief and related cognitive notions. This approach rules out the possibility that a speaker could recognize that two expressions are logically equivalent but distinct in meaning.

The second strategy involves using a non-antisymmetric preorder in the lattice of propositions to model the relation of entailment. This approach require formulating a proof theory in which provable equivalence does not entail identity.

In our survey of hyperintensionalist theories proposed in the post-Montague period we found that most proposals either adopt a version of an impossible worlds view, or leave their proof or their model theories crucially underspecified. In Chapters 4 and 5 we construct a higher-order and a first-order fine-grained intensional theory, respectively, using the non-antisymmetric preorder characterization of entailment. Each of these theories involves distinct choices concerning the design of the type system, expressibility within the object language, and the formal power of the logic.

Chapter 3

Intensions as Primitives

In this chapter we approach intensionality from what might be regarded as a slightly different perspective. Rather than considering how to fix existing proposals, we start by considering the essential requirements of an intensional theory. This is what we mean by 'primitive intensionality'; intensionality that is basic, and not defined in terms of other notions. First, we present a simple, untyped theory, UTIL, which provides a vehicle for considering the salient issues. Then we present a more sophisticated theory, PT, which addresses some of the shortcomings of UTIL. Finally, we reflect on some choices that have to be made, and constraints upon those choices.

This leads to a summary of the different approaches taken by FIL and PTCT, the two main theories introduced in this book. Both these theories take an axiomatic approach to hyperintensionalism, and assign model theory a secondary role. We define a class of models that provide a minimal model theory in which our logics are sound and which support counter-examples to the axiom of extensionality.

3.1 A Simple Intensional Theory

It is instructive to consider a very basic first-order logic which addresses one of the primary concerns, that of producing an account of intensionality. This initial language is called Untyped Intensional Logic (UTIL). It illustrates how fine-grained intensionality can be achieved in a simple logic. We can then observe why such a logic is inadequate as a basis for natural language semantics. This inadequacy results from the absence of a notion of types (or sorts), application and abstraction.

There are choices in how the shortcomings of a simple theory such as UTIL can be addressed. Many complications can arise when addressing these issues. The different choices, and the different solutions for addressing the complications that arise, lead to a range of logics. The remainder of the book presents two approaches to the problem. One, FIL, can be seen as offering a fairly conservative solution, essentially adapting a popular existing framework for semantics, in the form of Montague's (1974) IL, to produce a truly intensional system. The other, PTCT, offers a more radical approach, which maintains fine-grained intensionality, adds abstraction, application and types, while remaining in a first-order framework. In addition, a flexible type system is adopted which has strong linguistic motivation.

3.1.1 The Language UTIL

The simplest logic that allows us to investigate issues in intensionality must allow expressions $a, b, \ldots$ corresponding to propositions to appear as arguments in predicates and relations, as in $p(\ldots a \ldots)$. In an extensional theory, substituting an expression that represents or denotes a logically equivalent expression will always produce a logically equivalent statement. That is, if $a \leftrightarrow b$, then $p(\ldots a \ldots) \leftrightarrow p(\ldots b \ldots)$.

By contrast, an intensional theory will allow cases where syntactically distinct but logically equivalent expressions can be substituted without necessarily resulting in a logically equivalent statement. Informally speaking, the greater the range of differences in arguments a and b that fail to result in equivalences of the form $p(\ldots a \ldots) \leftrightarrow p(\ldots b \ldots)$, the more 'fine-grained' the intensionality of the theory.

Here we set up a theory UTIL that allows propositional expressions to appear as arguments, and which supports fine-grained intensionality. This shows that producing a theory that just supports an appropriate notion of intensionality is not particularly difficult. The problems will arise when we consider how the theory can be adapted to incorporate notions of type and function.

In the presentation adopted here, we choose to distinguish between propositional expressions that can appear as arguments, which we term *intensions*, and those that are used to make statements, which we term *wffs*. In this case, the distinction between intensions and wffs is somewhat redundant (unlike in PTCT, where it plays a central role in the formulation).[13]

We adopt a simplified Backus–Naur Form (BNF) notation for the presentation of the syntax.[14] In brief, the constant on the left side of ::= is used to refer to the category that is being defined, and the expressions on the right side of ::= present the various ways that category can be instantiated (or 'expanded'), with each possibility disjoined from the next by the | symbol. The definitions may be recursive, with the category name appearing on the right side.

The language consists of the following terms and well-formed formulae (wffs):

(58) Terms $t ::= c \mid x \mid I$

(59) Intensions $I ::= R_n(t_1, \ldots, t_n) \mid \neg I \mid I \wedge I \mid \forall x(I)$

(60) Wffs $\varphi ::= R_n(t_1, \ldots, t_n) \mid \neg\varphi \mid \varphi \wedge \varphi \mid \forall x(\varphi)$

[13] Although even with PTCT it would be possible to avoid using distinct languages of terms (intensions) and wffs by capturing the behavior of the logic more directly with deduction rules, rather than by way of the meta-language that is provided by the language of wffs.

[14] This notation was devised by John Backus and Peter Naur to describe the syntax of the programming language ALGOL (Naur 1960). By convention, BNF category names are surrounded by $\langle$ and $\rangle$. We ignore this convention here.

The wffs $\varphi \to \varphi, \varphi \leftrightarrow \varphi, \varphi \vee \varphi, \exists x(\varphi)$ can be defined in the usual way.

Here we have explicitly indicated that there are expressions I of a propositional form that can appear in a wff wherever a term can appear. That is, expressions of a propositional form, including relation symbols and logical constants, can appear as arguments of relation symbols R_n. The intention is that when interpreted as wffs, they are given an extensional interpretation, and when appearing as arguments of R_n, they are given an intensional interpretation, with a correspondingly weaker identity criteria.

In the above presentation, the syntax of the language restricts the form of intensional expressions to those that correspond to propositions: all expressions in I have the form of propositions. This is a standard approach in logics for natural language semantics, including the language FIL.

There is an alternative, where the syntax of the language is more open. Constraints on whether or not a term has the 'appropriate' form are given elsewhere, by way of additional rules or axioms.

(61) Terms $t ::= R_n \mid c \mid x \mid \neg \mid\wedge\mid \forall$

(62) Wffs $\varphi ::= \varphi \wedge \varphi \mid \neg\varphi \mid \forall x(\varphi) \mid R_n(t_1, \ldots, t_n)$

Here, arbitrary fragments of propositions can appear in all places that a term can appear. We could then consider adding a predicate (e.g. proposition′) to the wff which characterizes those terms that correspond to propositions. Schematically, this could be achieved with the following axioms:

(63) (a) proposition′$(R_n(t_1, \ldots, t_n))$
(b) proposition′$(I) \to$ proposition′$(\neg I)$
(c) proposition′$(I) \wedge$ proposition′$(I') \to$ proposition′$(I \wedge I')$
(d) $\forall x$(proposition′$(I)) \to$ proposition′$(\forall x(I))$

This is similar to the approach adopted in PTCT (and which is also employed in Turner's (1992) PT).

Alternatively, we could express these constraints as derivation rules, where the judgement t : Prop indicates that t is a proposition, as follows.

(64)

$$\frac{}{R_n(t_1, \ldots, t_n) : \text{Prop}}$$

$$\frac{I : \text{Prop}}{\neg I : \text{Prop}} \qquad \frac{I : \text{Prop} \quad I' : \text{Prop}}{I \wedge I' : \text{Prop}} \qquad \frac{I[x] : \text{Prop}}{\forall x(I) : \text{Prop}}$$

3.1.2 Sketch of a Model for UTIL

The role of a model is to show that there is an interpretation of the logic that supports the desired patterns of behaviour. First, we give a model for the terms, and then extend this to a model of the entire theory.

Terms can be given an intensional interpretation in a domain D by I_g, using an assignment function g, and a bijective interpretation function i, which (for example) assigns a Gödel numbering in D to constants c, logical constants $\wedge, \neg, \forall$ and relation symbols R_n of t. Here we take c' to include c and the logical constants $\wedge, \neg, \forall$. In the following, $\circ$ represents the operation that computes a unique integer from its arguments.

(65) (a) $I_g(c') = i(c')$
(b) $I_g(R_n) = i(R_n)$
(c) $I_g(x) = g(x)$
(d) $I_g(R_n(t_1, \ldots, t_n)) = I_g(R_n) \circ (I_g(t_1), \ldots, I_g(t_n))$
(e) $I_g(\neg\varphi) = I_g(\neg) \circ I_g(\varphi)$
(f) $I_g(\varphi \wedge \psi) = I_g(\wedge) \circ (I_g(\varphi), I_g(\psi))$
(g) $I_g(\forall x\varphi) = I_g(\forall) \circ (I_g(x), I_g(\varphi))$

Wffs can be given an extensional interpretation E_g, where the logical connectives have the standard interpretations, and each relation symbol R_n is interpreted by E as a subset of D^n.

(66) (a) $E_g(R_n(t_1, \ldots, t_n)) = (I_g(t_1), \ldots, I_g(t_n)) \in E(R_n)$
(b) $E_g(\neg\varphi) = 1$ iff $E_g(\varphi) = 0$
(c) $E_g(\varphi \wedge \psi) = 1$ iff $E_g(\varphi) = 1$ and $E_g(\psi) = 1$
(d) $E_g(\forall x\varphi) = 1$ iff $E_{g[d/x]}\varphi$ for all $d \in D$

As an alternative, we could define an extensional interpretation function E' that operates on the intensional interpretations of wffs, such that $E'(I_g(\varphi)) = E_g(\varphi)$.

3.1.3 Equality and Equivalence

We can define a distinguished two-place relation =, such that in the model, $E_g(t = s) = 1$ iff $I_g(t) = I_g(s)$ (adopting the usual infix notation). We can also defined equivalence $\leftrightarrow$ in the usual way, so that $E_g(\varphi \leftrightarrow \psi) = 1$ iff $E_g(\varphi) = 1$ exactly when $E_g(\psi) = 1$, that is, iff $E_g(\varphi) = E_g(\psi)$.

Now we can see that although $\varphi \leftrightarrow \psi$ follows from $\varphi = \psi$, the converse does not hold. One of the consequences of this can be seen by way of an example:

(67) $(\neg\varphi \vee \psi) \leftrightarrow (\varphi \rightarrow \psi)$

but it is not the case that

(68) $\mathsf{believe}_2'(john', (\neg\varphi \vee \psi)) \leftrightarrow \mathsf{believe}_2'(john', (\varphi \rightarrow \psi))$

Although a somewhat artificial example, this illustrates that UTIL captures the essence of a system with fine-grained intensionality as required for natural language. That is, a propositional attitude such as belief in a statement does not mean that the same attitude is held towards an equivalent statement. Of course, we might argue that if *john′* has a grounding in elementary logic, he will indeed believe $\varphi \rightarrow \psi$ whenever he believes $\neg\varphi \vee \psi$, but that is not the point: we can always add postulates to an individual's theory of belief that allows us to infer a belief in one statement given a belief in another.[15] The problem is having sufficiently fine-grained intensionality for us not to be required to equate such beliefs in all cases. Our semantic theory should, at its heart, allow for the most fine-grained of distinctions between expressions.

Although it serves as an illustration of an intensional theory, there are many shortcomings to this theory. In particular, there is no notion of functions, types, nor abstraction and application.

[15] Formulating such theories in FIL and PTCT would be worthwhile research projects.

3.2 Types and Sorts

As presented, UTIL does not impose any typing or sortal requirements on the arguments of propositions within the theory. In the example above, we cannot insist that the second argument of $\mathsf{believe}'_2$ is a proposition. However, as sketched above, it is possible to extend the theory with sorts, and define a sort proposition′ that holds terms that correspond with syntactically well-formed propositions. The theory could be further extended with functions and function sorts.

As things stand, there is a slight problem with this proposal. The sortal constraints would be expressed in the language of wffs, and would govern the sorting of the arguments within intensional expressions, but UTIL lacks the means to express sortal constraints giving well-formedness conditions on the wffs themselves. For example, although we could express the constraint that p in the term $\mathsf{believe}'_2(mary', p)$ should be a proposition for the entire expression to be a proposition, we cannot express this constraint when $\mathsf{believe}'_2(mary', p)$ is a wff.

There are a range of solutions to this. One option is to go to a full higher-order regime, where typing constraints are imposed directly on the syntax of the language of wffs. Propositions can then appear as arguments of predicates and relations if the type of those predicates and relations allows a proposition to appear at the appropriate argument position. This approach is adopted in FIL. Unfortunately, this results in a theory that is not recursively enumerable. Also, the rigid Church-style syntactic typing (Church 1940) results in some inflexibility which is arguably at odds with the requirements of natural language semantics.

An alternative option is to represent all propositions, relations and predicates in a syntactically 'flat' intensional language of terms, and then allow an independent system of sorts or types to be imposed on these representations. This gives rise to flexible, Curry-style typing. We further have to be able to determine the truth conditions of terms representing propositions, either by adding inference rules with truth judgements, or by adding a truth predicate to relate those term representations to truth conditions expressed in some meta-language of wffs. A variant of this latter approach is adopted in PTCT.

There are other options for developing typed logics, and other issues that we have not considered here, such as whether or not the types should be stratified. Some of these points are discussed in more detail by Turner (1997, 2004).

3.3 Abstraction and Application

One reason for desiring abstraction and application is that it enables semantic expressions to be composed. Although it is perhaps not an essential requirement of a theory for computational semantics that the process of composition be conducted within the theory itself, conventionally it is seen as desirable to consider the fragments of semantic interpretation associated with non-sentential phrases as carriers of meaning that can receive an interpretation within a single theory.

The λ-calculus (in all its forms) provides a vehicle for expressing functions and function application. By adopting a version of the λ-calculus, a semantic theory gains the possibility of expressing derived functions (by way of abstraction) and the corresponding functional types. The abstraction and application of λ-calculus provide a means of including the derivation of semantic representations within the theory. These reasons provide motivation for exploring intensional theories that embody versions of the λ-calculus.

FIL adopts a simply typed $\lambda\alpha\beta$-calculus in the language of wffs, following Church (1940), where, for example, the types of the calculus determine which expressions are the bearers of truth in extensional contexts. Conceptually, it builds upon existing type-theoretic logics. In contrast, PTCT incorporates the untyped λ-calculus into its language of terms. Typing constraints are expressed in the Curry-style. This can be conceived of as a development of Turner's (1992) Property Theory (PT).

3.4 PT: An Untyped Theory

One way in which we could improve on UTIL is to adopt PT, Turner's axiomatization of Aczel's Frege Structures (Aczel 1980; Turner 1992).[16] PT's language of terms is that of the untyped λ-calculus augmented with logical constants that represent the logical operators.

In PT well-formedness conditions are expressed as semantic (logical) constraints rather than being described syntactically. This approach will also be adopted in PTCT. In the case of PT, typing constraints are expressed sortally. The untyped λ-calculus adopted by PTpermits self-application. Without care, logical theories that permit self-application run the risk of inconsistency, as we can produce representations of paradoxical assertions. To see this, consider the term R defined by

(69) $R = \lambda x(\sim xx)$

It is easy to see that $RR = \sim RR$ by substitution and β-reduction. If we allow the expression RR to be a proposition, then we have a version of Russell's paradox, namely $RR \leftrightarrow \sim RR$, which is of the form $a \leftrightarrow \sim a$. To avoid such problems, there must be constraints on when it is permissible to consider the truth-conditions of terms. PT avoids this problem by having only a subset of terms to represent felicitous propositions. PT's language of terms contains a predicate Prop that holds only of terms that represent propositions, and only propositions have truth conditions. Rather than impose a syntax on the propositional terms, Prop is used to characterize meaningful terms, much like proposition′ in UTIL.

3.4.1 Formalization of PT

Here we give a sketch of a version of PT with a minimal number of logical constants and operators. Conceptually, it resembles UTIL,

[16] This presentation is provided for completeness. PT provides the foundation upon which PTCT is built. Readers who are not interested in the details of PT may wish to skip directly to the discussion of PTCT.

augmented by abstraction and application. In addition, a truth predicate allows us to characterize those terms that represent true propositions.

(70) Terms $t ::= c \mid x \mid l \mid t(t) \mid \lambda x(t)$

(71) Logical constants $l ::= \hat{\sim} \mid \hat{\wedge} \mid \hat{\forall} \mid \hat{=}$

(72) Wffs $\varphi ::= \varphi \wedge \varphi \mid \sim \varphi \mid \forall x(\varphi) \mid \mathsf{Prop}(t) \mid \mathsf{True}(t) \mid t = t'$

The terms are governed by the $\lambda\alpha\beta$-calculus.[17]

(73) $\lambda x(t) =_{\alpha} \lambda y(t[x/y])$ where y is not free in t

(74) $(\lambda x(t))t' =_{\beta} t[x/t']$ where t' is not free in t

The logical constants are taken to be represented by terms of the λ-calculus. In the case of felicitous propositions, these connectives appear in a prefix position. However, we adopt an infix notation for clarity. For example, $((\hat{\wedge})t)t'$ will be written $(t \mathbin{\hat{\wedge}} t')$. Similary, in the case of the term representation of quantified expressions, rather than writing $(\hat{\forall})(\lambda x.t)$ we shall write $\hat{\forall}x(t)$.

The logical operators $\exists, \vee, \rightarrow, \leftrightarrow$ and the terms $\hat{\exists}, \hat{\vee}, \hat{\rightarrow}, \hat{\leftrightarrow}$ can either be added explicitly, or definitionally, using the conventional definitions and their intensional analogues.

We wish $\mathsf{Prop}(t)$ to follow for any term t that represents a felicitous proposition. The predicate Prop, and hence the notion of proposition, is governed by the following axioms:

(75) (a) $\mathsf{Prop}(p) \rightarrow \mathsf{Prop}(\hat{\sim} p)$
(b) $(\mathsf{Prop}(p) \wedge \mathsf{Prop}(q)) \rightarrow \mathsf{Prop}(p \mathbin{\hat{\wedge}} q)$
(c) $\forall x \mathsf{Prop}(p) \rightarrow \mathsf{Prop}(\hat{\forall}x(p))$
(d) $\mathsf{True}(p) \rightarrow \mathsf{Prop}(p)$
(e) $\mathsf{Prop}(t \mathbin{\hat{=}} t')$

17 In PT we assume that η (namely, $\lambda u(tu) = t$) does not hold, as this leads to intensional collapse. However, we are able to incorporate versions of η into PTCT and FIL without incurring this result.

The wff $\mathsf{True}(t)$ will be applicable to any term t that is a proposition, and will lead to a wff that is true in the event t represents a true proposition. Here we axiomatize truth for those terms that are propositions.

(76) (a) $\mathsf{Prop}(p) \rightarrow \mathsf{True}(\hat{\sim} p) \leftrightarrow {\sim}\mathsf{True}(p)$
(b) $(\mathsf{Prop}(p) \wedge \mathsf{Prop}(q)) \rightarrow (\mathsf{True}(p \mathbin{\hat{\wedge}} q) \leftrightarrow (\mathsf{True}(p) \wedge \mathsf{True}(q)))$
(c) $\forall x \mathsf{Prop}(p) \rightarrow \mathsf{True}(\hat{\forall} x(p)) \leftrightarrow \forall x(\mathsf{True}(p))$
(d) $\mathsf{True}(t \mathbin{\hat{=}} t') \leftrightarrow (t = t')$

3.4.2 'Types' in PT

Apart from the notion of a proposition, PT does not have any types as such. However, it is possible to mimic types using sortal predicates. In this way, various types, and type operators can be defined, including the type operators of constructive type theories such as Martin-Löf Type Theory (MLTT).

Relations and predicates are then represented by terms that give rise to atomic propositions when given the appropriate number of arguments. We can think of adding a system of sorts that allow us to indicate the number of arguments (and perhaps their sort) that a term requires in order to produce a proposition. For example, a property will require just one term:

(77) $\mathsf{Pty}(p) =_{\mathsf{def}} \forall x(\mathsf{Prop}(px))$

Following Turner (1992), we can define the notion of an n-place relation:

(78) (a) $\mathsf{Rel}_0(t) =_{\mathsf{def}} \mathsf{Prop}(t)$
(b) $\mathsf{Rel}_n(t) =_{\mathsf{def}} \forall x \mathsf{Rel}_{n-1}(tx)$

We can also define general function space sorts $(S \Longrightarrow T)$:

(79) $(S \Longrightarrow T)(t) =_{\mathsf{def}} \forall x(S(x) \rightarrow T(tx))$

Using the syntactic sugar of $\{x.t\}$ for $\lambda x(t)$, and $x \epsilon t$ for $\mathsf{True}(tx)$, we can mimic a system of types:

(80)
$$\begin{aligned}
\cap &=_{\text{def}} \lambda f \lambda g\{x.fx \mathbin{\hat{\wedge}} gx\}\\
\cup &=_{\text{def}} \lambda f \lambda g\{x.fx \mathbin{\hat{\vee}} gx\}\\
- &=_{\text{def}} \lambda f \lambda g\{x.fx \mathbin{\hat{\wedge}} \hat{\sim} gx\}\\
\otimes &=_{\text{def}} \lambda f \lambda g\{z.\hat{\exists} x \hat{\exists} y(z \mathrel{\hat{=}} \langle x, y\rangle \mathbin{\hat{\wedge}} fx \mathbin{\hat{\wedge}} gy)\}\\
\oplus &=_{\text{def}} \lambda f \lambda g\{z.(\mathsf{fst}(z) \mathrel{\hat{=}} 0 \mathbin{\hat{\wedge}} f(\mathsf{snd}(z))) \mathbin{\hat{\vee}} (\mathsf{fst}(z) \mathrel{\hat{=}} 1 \mathbin{\hat{\wedge}}\\
&\qquad\qquad g(\mathsf{snd}(z)))\}\\
\mapsto &=_{\text{def}} \lambda f \lambda g\{z.\hat{\forall} x(fx \mathrel{\hat{\rightarrow}} g(zx))\}
\end{aligned}$$

which trivially lead to the following theorems:

(81)
$$\begin{aligned}
z\varepsilon(t \cap s) &\leftrightarrow z\varepsilon t \wedge z\varepsilon s\\
z\varepsilon(t \cup s) &\leftrightarrow z\varepsilon t \vee z\varepsilon s\\
z\varepsilon(t - s) &\leftrightarrow z\varepsilon t \wedge {\sim} z\varepsilon s\\
z\varepsilon(t \otimes s) &\leftrightarrow \mathsf{fst}(z)\varepsilon t \wedge \mathsf{snd}(z)\varepsilon s\\
z\varepsilon(t \oplus s) &\leftrightarrow (\mathsf{fst}(z) = 0 \wedge \mathsf{snd}(z)\varepsilon t) \vee (\mathsf{fst}(z) = 1 \wedge \mathsf{snd}(z)\varepsilon s)\\
z\varepsilon(t \mapsto s) &\leftrightarrow \forall x(x\varepsilon t \rightarrow zx\varepsilon s)
\end{aligned}$$

where pairs $\langle \cdot, \cdot \rangle$ and the projection, or selector functions fst, snd have their usual definitions:

(82)
$$\begin{aligned}
\langle x, y\rangle &=_{\text{def}} \lambda z(z(x)(y))\\
\mathsf{fst} &=_{\text{def}} \lambda p(p\lambda xy(x))\\
\mathsf{snd} &=_{\text{def}} \lambda p(p\lambda xy(y))
\end{aligned}$$

so that:

(83)
$$\begin{aligned}
\mathsf{fst}\langle x, y\rangle &=_{\beta} x\\
\mathsf{snd}\langle x, y\rangle &=_{\beta} y
\end{aligned}$$

3.4.3 A Universal Type in PT

We can add a universal type Δ to PT such that

(84) $\forall x(x \in \Delta)$

This makes it possible to apply Chierchia's analysis of nominalization (Chierchia 1982). Phrases such as *is fun* can take nouns, gerunds and infinitives as arguments, as in:

(85) (a) Tennis is fun.

(b) Playing tennis is fun.
(c) To play tennis is fun.

Following Chierchia, these examples can be accounted for by saying, in effect, that the representation of *fun* is of the type $\Delta \Longrightarrow$ Prop. That is, the representation of *fun* yields a proposition for any argument. This would also allow us to account for apparent cases of self-predication, as in *fun is fun*.

Having a universal type also allows for an analysis of natural language conjunction, which is not restricted to conjoining phrases of any particular category. Chierchia observes that this can be dealt with by giving the representation of conjunction the type $\Delta \Longrightarrow (\Delta \Longrightarrow \Delta)$.

3.4.4 Dependent Types in PT

Although we do not exploit such types, it is instructive to observe that dependent type operators corresponding to those used in MLTT can be defined in PT as follows:

(86) $\Sigma =_{\mathsf{def}} \lambda f \lambda g\{h : f(\mathsf{fst}(h)) \mathbin{\hat{\wedge}} g(\mathsf{fst}(h))(\mathsf{snd}(h))\}$

(87) $\Pi =_{\mathsf{def}} \lambda f \lambda g\{h : \hat{\forall} x(fx \mathbin{\hat{\rightarrow}} gx(hx)\}$

These definitions support the following theorems:

(88) If $\mathsf{Pty}(f)$ and $\forall x(x\varepsilon f \rightarrow \mathsf{Pty}(gx))$ then:

$$\mathsf{Pty}(\Sigma f g)$$
$$\mathsf{Pty}(\Pi f g)$$

(89) $h\varepsilon\Sigma fg \leftrightarrow \mathsf{fst}(h)\varepsilon f \wedge \mathsf{snd}(h)\varepsilon g(\mathsf{fst}(h))$

(90) $h\varepsilon\Pi fg \leftrightarrow \forall x(x\varepsilon f \rightarrow hx\varepsilon gx)$

This mimics the work of Smith (1984) which shows how to interpret MLTT within a Frege Structure (Aczel 1980): PT is essentially an axiomatization of a Frege Structure, and these definitions give a mapping from MLTT into this classical theory. There have been proposals for using types such as these as a vehicle for interpreting natural language discourse (Dávila-Pérez 1994, 1995; Sundholm 1989), or for generating natural language discourse from such type expressions (Ranta 1991, 1994).

3.4.5 Internal Definability

A predicate Q in the language of wff is said to be *internally definable* iff there is a property q such that:

(91) $\forall x(Q(x) \leftrightarrow x \varepsilon q)$

That is, $\forall x(Q(x) \leftrightarrow \mathsf{True}(qx))$.

Note that neither True nor Prop are internally definable, as that would lead to a paradox (Aczel 1980; Turner 1990). For example, assuming that we can internally define True by the property true′, then the following holds:

(92) (a) $\mathsf{Prop}(\mathsf{true}'(t))$, for all t, as true′ is a property.
(b) $\forall x(\mathsf{True}(x) \leftrightarrow \mathsf{True}(\mathsf{true}'(x)))$ from the definition of internal definability.
(c) $\forall x(\mathsf{True}(\hat{\sim}\,\mathsf{true}'(x)) \leftrightarrow {\sim}\,\mathsf{True}(\mathsf{true}'(x)))$ from the axioms of PT, given that true′ is a property.

Now we can define a term r as follows:

(93) $r =_{\mathsf{def}} \lambda x(\hat{\sim}\,\mathsf{true}'(xx))$

and consider the expression rr:

(94) $rr = (\lambda x(\hat{\sim}\,\mathsf{true}'(xx)))\lambda x(\hat{\sim}\,\mathsf{true}'(xx))$
$= \hat{\sim}\,\mathsf{true}'((\lambda x(\hat{\sim}\,\mathsf{true}'(xx)))\lambda x(\hat{\sim}\,\mathsf{true}'(xx)))$
$= \hat{\sim}\,\mathsf{true}'(rr)$

We can then deduce that:

(95) $\mathsf{True}(\hat{\sim}\,\mathsf{true}'(rr)) \leftrightarrow {\sim}\,\mathsf{True}(rr)$

But $rr = \hat{\sim}\,\mathsf{true}'(rr)$, so we can deduce:

(96) $\text{True}(\hat{\sim}\text{true}'(rr)) \leftrightarrow \sim\text{True}(rr)$
$\leftrightarrow \sim\text{True}(\hat{\sim}\text{true}'(rr))$

which is a contradiction, and so True cannot be internally definable. Similar arguments can be made in the case of Prop.

However, predicates that do not lead to the internalization of Prop and True can be defined internally. For example, we can introduce internally definable classes of individual. These can be used when formulating notions of plural individual and natural language denotable individuals (Fox 2000). Types which are characterized by such internally definable predicates are also known as 'small types' (Aczel 1980).

We can introduce internal analogues to Prop and True in PT, provided they cannot be shown to be properties. For example, we can have $\mathfrak{prop}$, $\mathfrak{true}$ where:

(97) (a) $\text{Prop}(s) \rightarrow \text{Prop}(\mathfrak{prop}(s))$
(b) $\text{Prop}(s) \rightarrow \text{Prop}(\mathfrak{true}(s))$
(c) $\text{Prop}(s) \rightarrow (\text{True}(\mathfrak{prop}(s)) \leftrightarrow \text{Prop}(s))$
(d) $\text{Prop}(s) \rightarrow (\text{True}(\mathfrak{true}(s)) \leftrightarrow \text{True}(s))$

These terms behave like **S5** modalities (Turner 1990).

3.4.6 Strengths and Weaknesses of PT

PT is a good candidate for a theory for natural language semantics. It has fine-grained intensionality, flexible sorting/types, and can capture MLTT, which could be applied to analyze some discourse phenomena. It also allows felicitous cases of self-application, although it is not immediately clear whether this is essential for natural language semantics.

However, there are some drawbacks. The core notions of the theory, those of truth, and of proposition, are not internally definable. This might lead to problems if we wish to constrain the domain of quantification to propositions, for example, as might be appropriate in sentences such as *John believes everything Mary believes* when they appear in intensional contexts (Section 9.4). Furthermore, although PT supports a universal type, this is a rather coarse analysis of polymorphism in natural language. For example, in the case of conjunction, using the type $\Delta \Longrightarrow (\Delta \Longrightarrow \Delta)$ fails to express the fact that the conjuncts and the resultant conjoined expressions are all expected to be of the same type.

Because Prop and True cannot be internalized, PT is characterized as a *stratified* theory. If it is important to be able to internalize well-formedness criteria, then we can adopt an unstratified theory (such as PTCT). Alternatively, it is possible to define a stratified hierarchy of languages in which each language can internalize the notion of proposition in languages below it in the hierarchy (Turner 2004). Unlike PTCT, this latter approach permits felicitous cases of self-application.

In passing, we note that in addition to Aczel's (1980) work on Frege Structures, and Turner's (1992) axiomatization of them, there have been many other proposals for a property-theoretic approach to fine-grained intensionality, including, but not limited to, Cocchiarella (1979), Kamareddine (1995), and of course Bealer (1982), the last of which was discussed in Section 2.4.

3.5 Intensionality in FIL and PTCT

Montague's (1974) IL uses a formal trick to allow us to consider a wff as an argument of a predicate. One role this plays is to work around an issue in the rigid, Church-style typing he employs (Church 1940).

Even in intensional contexts, the mapping from natural language to wffs is essentially extensional in character (where a proposition is an extensional function from possible worlds to truth). Unfortunately, the equivalence criteria given by such functions is not sufficiently fine-grained for natural language semantics. For example, necessary truths, such as those of mathematics, become equated, along with propositional attitudes towards them.

In contrast, FIL addresses this issue by adopting a distinct intensional interpretation for wffs in opaque contexts. The theory then has two distinct notions of equality, one of extensional equivalence, and another of intensional identity. In the absence of additional meaning postulates, only expressions that are intensionally identical may be freely substituted into opaque contexts. FIL maintains the essential aspects of the simple type theory of Montague's IL. It can then be seen as a formal fix to one of IL's shortcomings.

PTCT adopts a different approach to producing fine-grained intensionality. It is based upon the observation that any logical theory with equality already has much of the machinery required to produce a theory with notions of extensional equivalence and intensional identity. First, the language of wffs already provides extensional notions of equivalence for propositions and predicates. Propositions are equivalent if they are true (false) together, and predicates are equivalent if they have the same membership. Second, the language of terms has a distinct notion of identity, given by the equality of terms.

Rather than amend the model of wffs in an intensional context so they have the appropriate logical behaviour, PTCT identifies the logic of intensions with the logic of terms. Without additional meaning postulates, this logic is simply one of intensional identity.

Rather than translating directly into a language of wffs, natural language is translated into a language of terms, enriched with appropriate constants to *represent* propositions. Those terms that represent propositions can then be given truth conditions in the language of wffs. Intensional identity is then term equality, and extensional equivalence is given by way of logical equivalence of the truth conditions (or membership criteria, in the case of predicates) in the language of wffs.

3.6 Conclusion

The notion of fine-grained intensionality is not in itself difficult to capture. Difficulties arise when we consider how to combine fine-grained intensionality with a notion of functions, abstraction, application and systems of types. Without care, paradoxes and inconsistencies can arise.

There are different ways in which such paradoxes can be avoided. We can either ban self-application by adopting a typed λ-calculus that does not permit it, as in FIL, or we can allow self-application, but limit the kinds of expressions that can be considered to represent propositions. It is possible to formulate theories in which non-problematic instances of self-application can represent propositions. This is the approach taken by PT, for example. This can be contrasted with PTCT, which in principle allows self-application, but does not allow any such terms to represent propositions. The reward for this apparent limitation is that PTCT allows more significant parts of the type system to be internalized, so that we can have intensional representations of typed quantification.

The nature of the type system, and how it is formulated, provide another dimension of choice in devising a semantic framework, although the choice is constrained somewhat by the approach taken to the paradoxes that can arise from self-application. The precise formulation of the type system governs the formal power of the logic. PT adopts a first-order sortal system of types. Only some of the types can safely be represented in the intensional language. Unlike PT, both PTCT and FIL allow intensional representations of typed quantification, but PTCT achieves this in a first-order framework.

When considered in isolation, it is difficult to make judgements about the merits of the various approaches to intensionality, self-application, types and formal power. Here, we are motivated by empirical considerations of natural language, its semantics, and the desire to have a system that supports effective reasoning.

Chapter 4

A Higher-Order, Fine-Grained Intensional Logic

This chapter describes a higher-order logic with fine-grained intensionality (FIL). Unlike traditional Montogovian type theory, intensionality is treated as basic, rather than derived through possible worlds. This allows for fine-grained intensionality without impossible worlds. Possible worlds and modalities are defined algebraically. The proof theory for FIL is given as a set of tableau rules, and an algebraic model theory is specified. The proof theory is shown to be sound relative to this model theory. FIL avoids many of the problems created by classical coarse-grained intensional logics that have been used in formal and computational semantics.

In a sense, FIL can be thought of as a reformulation of MS (Chapter 1.1). It is for this reason that we include a treatment of modality; so as to make it very clear that modality and intensionality are not conflated.

4.1 Introduction

It has frequently been noted that the characterization of intensions as functions from indices to denotations, as in Montague (1974), yields a semantics which is not sufficiently fine-grained. For example, logically equivalent expressions are co-intensional and thus intersubstitutable in all contexts, including the complements of propositional attitude predicates. The view that expressions are co-intensional just in case they have the same denotation across indices has been dominant in formal semantics since at least Carnap (1947).

An alternative view, which we refer to as *hyperintensionalism*, posits propositions as independent intensional entities, and takes truth to be a derived relational property. In the past twenty years a variety of hyperintensionalist theories have been proposed, including Thomason (1980), situation semantics (Barwise and Etchemendy 1990; Barwise and Perry 1983; Seligman and Moss 1997), Landman (1986b), property theory (Chierchia and Turner 1988; Turner 1987, 1992), Muskens (1995), and Lappin and Pollard (1999). With the exception of Turner (1992), these theories have focused on the interpretative structures while remaining inexplicit or programmatic about the logic.

We depart from this tradition by constructing an explicit proof theory for a fine-grained logic and then defining a class of models in which the logic is sound. The logic is broadly similar to Church's (1940) simple theory of types (STT), augmented with a coextensionality predicate. It differs crucially from more familiar elaborations of STT (such as Henkin (1950) and Gallin (1975)) in having models that falsify the axiom of propositional extensionality.

4.2 Fine-Grained Intensional Logic

Fine-Grained Intensional Logic (FIL), like STT, incorporates the typed λ-calculus into a classical logic.

4.2.1 The Set of Types

We define the set of types in our fine-grained intensional logic FIL as follows:

The Types

(98) Basic Types
   (a) i (*individual concepts*)
   (b) p (propositions)

(99) Exponential Types
   If A, B are types, then A^B is a type.

This is the type system of Church (1940). Unlike Gallin's (1975) Ty2, there is no additional type s for possible worlds. For each type A there is (i) a (possibly non-empty) denumerable set of non-logical constants of type A; and (ii) a denumerably infinite set of variables of type A. The constants serve as logical translations of words in a natural language whose semantic structure is being represented.

We define the set E_A of expressions of type A as follows:

(100) (a) Every variable of type A is in E_A.
   (b) Every constant of type A is in E_A.
   (c) If $\alpha \in E_A$ and u is a variable in E_B, then $\lambda u\alpha \in E_{A^B}$.
   (d) If $\alpha \in E_{B^A}$ and $\beta \in E_A$, then $\alpha(\beta) \in E_B$.
   (e) If $\alpha, \beta \in E_A$, then $\alpha = \beta \in E_p$.
   (f) if $\alpha, \beta \in E_A$, then $\alpha \cong \beta \in E_p$.
   (g) $\top$ and $\bot \in E_p$.
   (h) If $\varphi, \psi \in E_p$, then so are
      i. $\sim\varphi$
      ii. $\varphi \vee \psi$
      iii. $\varphi \wedge \psi$
      iv. $\varphi \rightarrow \psi$
      v. $\varphi \leftrightarrow \psi$
   (i) If $\varphi \in E_p$ and u is a variable in E_A, then $\forall u\varphi$ and $\exists u\varphi \in E_p$.
   (j) If $\varphi \in E_p$, then $\Box\varphi$ and $\Diamond\varphi \in E_p$.

4.2.2 A Proof Theory for FIL

We formulate our proof theory for FIL as a set of tableau rules. We follow Fitting (2000), and Fitting and Mendelsohn (1999) in using prefixed rules, where a prefix σ is a positive integer that corresponds to a possible world.[18] A prefixed formula $\sigma : \varphi$ is interpreted as φ is true at σ ($\varphi \in w$, w the world corresponding to σ).

There are four general kinds of rules, A, B, C, and D. The symbol $*$ following a premise indicates that it has been used in the course of a proof and is no longer available for further application of tableau rules.

A-**Rule**

$$\begin{array}{c} A^* \\ | \\ A_1 \\ A_2 \end{array}$$

B-**Rule**

$$\begin{array}{ccc} & B^* & \\ \swarrow & & \searrow \\ B_1 & & B_2 \end{array}$$

C(*d*)-**Rule**

$$\begin{array}{c} C \\ | \\ C[d/x] \end{array}$$

where d occurs on the path (or is the only constant occurring in the path), and d, x are of the same type

D(*d*)-**Rule**

$$\begin{array}{c} D^* \\ | \\ D[d/x] \end{array}$$

where d does not occur previously on the path, and d, x are of the same type

In addition, there are also closure rules which indicate when a branch is *closed* due to a contradiction. To be specific, a path P of a tree is *closed* iff (i) P contains both a labelled formula $\sigma : \varphi$ and its negation $\sigma : \sim\varphi$, or (ii) P contains $\sigma : \bot$. P is *open* iff it is not closed. A proof of φ is a tree Tr with $1 : \sim\varphi$ at the root of Tr and all the branches of Tr are closed.

When a rule requires more than one premis, the premises are separated by commas. We suppress type subscripts in the rules where the type of an expression is obvious, or not relevant to the rule.

18 In our model theory for FIL we define a possible world as an ultra filter of the Boolean prelattice of propositions.

All the following rules apply for any prefix σ.

Top

$$\frac{\sigma : \sim\top}{\sigma : \bot}$$

Conjunction

$$\frac{\sigma : (s \wedge t)^*}{\begin{array}{c}\sigma : s\\ \sigma : t\end{array}}$$

Negated Conjunction

$$\frac{\sigma : \sim(s \wedge t)^*}{\sigma : \sim s \quad \mid \quad \sigma : \sim t}$$

Disjunction

$$\frac{\sigma : (s \vee t)^*}{\sigma : s \quad \mid \quad \sigma : t}$$

Negated Disjunction

$$\frac{\sigma : \sim(s \vee t)^*}{\begin{array}{c}\sigma : \sim s\\ \sigma : \sim t\end{array}}$$

Implication

$$\frac{\sigma : (s \rightarrow t)^*}{\sigma : \sim s \quad \mid \quad \sigma : t}$$

Negated Implication

$$\frac{\sigma : \sim(s \rightarrow t)^*}{\begin{array}{c}\sigma : s\\ \sigma : \sim t\end{array}}$$

Bi-Implication

$$\frac{\sigma : (s \leftrightarrow t)^*}{\begin{array}{c}\sigma : s\\ \sigma : t\end{array} \quad \mid \quad \begin{array}{c}\sigma : \sim s\\ \sigma : \sim t\end{array}}$$

Negated Bi-Implication

$$\frac{\sigma : \sim(s \leftrightarrow t)^*}{\begin{array}{c}\sigma : s\\ \sigma : \sim t\end{array} \quad \mid \quad \begin{array}{c}\sigma : \sim s\\ \sigma : t\end{array}}$$

Boolean Negation

$$\frac{\sigma : \sim\sim s^*}{\sigma : s}$$

Negated Quantification

$$\frac{\sigma : \sim Qu\varphi^*}{\sigma : Q'u \sim \varphi}$$

where Q' is the dual of Q

Universal Quantification

$$\frac{\sigma : \forall u\varphi}{\sigma : \varphi[\alpha/u]}$$

where (i) α is grounded, and (ii) α occurs on the path (or α is a new constant in the path)[19]

Existential Quantification

$$\frac{\sigma : \exists u\varphi^*}{\sigma : \varphi[\beta/u]}$$

where β is a new constant that does not occur on the path and $\beta, u \in A$

Identity

$$\frac{\sigma : \varphi}{\sigma : \varphi[\alpha/\beta]}$$

where $\sigma : \alpha = \beta$ is on the path

Non-Identity

$$\frac{\sigma : \sim(\alpha = \alpha)}{\sigma : \bot}$$

α-reduction

$$\frac{\sigma : \varphi}{\sigma : \varphi'}$$

where φ' is obtained from φ by substituting variables of the appropriate type that appear in the path for corresponding bound variables in φ

β-reduction

$$\frac{\sigma : \ldots(\lambda u\varphi)(\alpha)\ldots}{\sigma : \ldots\varphi[\alpha/u]\ldots}$$

α not bound in φ

η-reduction[20]

$$\frac{\sigma : \ldots\lambda u(\varphi u)\ldots}{\sigma : \ldots\varphi\ldots}$$

u not free in φ

19 A term is grounded in the sense of Fitting (2000) iff it is a closed term (constant, closed λ term, or closed formula) with a prefix σ.

20 η-reduction permits us to prove EXT of Church (1940): $\vdash \forall f, g(\forall u(f(u) = g(u)) \rightarrow f = g)$. As the antecedent of EXT requires intensional identity of $f(u)$ and $g(u)$ for every u, it does not compromise the intensionality of FIL. Specifically, it does not entail $\forall u, v_{\in A}(u \cong v \rightarrow u = v)$. We are grateful to Paul Gilmore for pointing this out to us.

Equivalence (1)

$$\sigma : \sim(\alpha \cong \alpha)$$
$$\sigma : \bot$$

Equivalence (2)

$$\sigma : \sim(\beta \cong \alpha)$$
$$\sigma : \bot$$

where $\sigma : (\alpha \cong \beta)$ *is on the path*

Equivalence (3)

$$\sigma : (\alpha \cong \beta)$$
$$\sigma : (\alpha \cong \gamma)$$

where $\sigma : (\beta \cong \gamma)$ *is on the path*

Equivalence (4)

$$\sigma : (s \cong t)^*$$

$\sigma : s$	$\sigma : \sim s$
$\sigma : t$	$\sigma : \sim t$

Co-extensionality (1)

$$\sigma : (\varphi \cong \psi)$$
$$\sigma : (\varphi(\alpha) \cong \psi(\alpha))$$

where $\varphi, \psi \in B^A$, $\alpha \in A$, *and* α *is a grounded term that appears in the path*

Co-extensionality (2)

$$\sigma : \sim(\varphi \cong \psi)^*$$
$$\sigma : \sim(\varphi(\beta) \cong \psi(\beta))$$

$\varphi, \psi \in B^A$, $\beta \in A$, *and* β *is a new constant that does not appear in the path*

Negated Modality

$$\sigma : \sim M\varphi^*$$
$$\sigma : M' \sim \varphi$$

where M *and* M' *are modal operators, and* M' *is the dual of* M

Modality □ S5

$$\sigma : \Box s$$
$$\sigma' : s$$

where σ' *is a prefix integer that appears in the path*

Modality ◇ S5

$$\sigma : \Diamond s^*$$
$$\sigma' : s$$

where σ' *is a new prefix integer that does not appear in the path*

Tableau proof methods for other modal logics can be defined by modifying and adding to the rules for the modal operators, as in Fitting and Mendelsohn (1999).

4.2.3 Distinguishing Between Equivalence and Identity

The relation = corresponds to identity of intension, while ≅ is interpreted as extensional equivalence of entities of the same type.[21] The tableau rules allow us to prove **IDENT** but not **EXTEN**.

IDENT: $\forall u, v_{\in A}(u = v \to u \cong v)$
EXTEN: $\forall u, v_{\in A}(u \cong v \to u = v)$

The proof for **IDENT** is as follows.
$1 : \sim \forall u, v_{\in A}(u = v \to u \cong v)^*$
$1 : \exists u, v_{\in A} \sim(u = v \to u \cong v)^*$ (Negated Quantification)
$1 : \sim(a = b \to a \cong b)^*$ (Existential Quantification)
$1 : a = b$
$1 : \sim(a \cong b)$ (Negated Implication)
$1 : \sim(a \cong a)$ (Identity)
$1 : \bot$ (Equivalence (1))
The tree is closed. The following tableau provides a counterexample to **EXTEN**:
$1 : \sim \forall u, v_{\in A}(u \cong v \to u = v)^*$
$1 : \exists u, v_{\in A} \sim(u \cong v \to u = v)^*$ (Negated Quantification)
$1 : \sim(a \cong b \to a = b)^*$ (Existential Quantification)
$1 : a \cong b$
$1 : \sim(a = b)$ (Negated Implication)
The tree is finished and open.

The proof theory for FIL entails that two expressions can be logically equivalent but not co-intensional, and so distinct propositions can imply each other.

It is worth noting that the proof of the invalidity of **EXTEN** establishes the consistency of the tableau rules for FIL. It

21 Within the framework of program specification theory, Maibaum (1997) discusses the use of a weak non-logical equality predicate to express the equivalence/congruence of possibly distinct expressions within a theory. Gilmore (2001) constructs an intensional simple theory of types (ITT) in which an intensional (=) and an extensional ($=_e$) identity predicate are defined. His proposal differs from that of Fox and Lappin (2001) and the current version of FIL in that (i) his extensional identity predicate is not type general, but is only defined for propositions and predicates, and (ii) for us identity and equivalence are primitive, whereas Gilmore defines them in terms of substitution and bi-implication.

demonstrates that not every sentence of FIL is provable, and so the proof theory for FIL is consistent.

4.3 A Semantics for FIL

4.3.1 Intensional Models

Before defining our class of models, we first review the notions of a frame and a Boolean prelattice, in terms of which these models will be specified. We take a *(Henkin) frame* to be a type-indexed family of sets $S = \langle S_A \rangle$ such that S_{C^B} is a (possibly proper) subset of the set of functions from S_B to S_C. We take a *Boolean prelattice* to be a set B with a preorder (a relation that is transitive, reflexive, but not antisymmetric) $\sqsubseteq$, two nullary operations T and F, one unary operation $'$ (written postfix), and four binary operations $\sqcap$, $\sqcup$, $\Rightarrow$, $\Leftrightarrow$, subject to the following conditions (here $\equiv$ is the relation on B such that $a \equiv b$ iff $a \sqsubseteq b$ and $b \sqsubseteq a$).[22]

(101) (a) T is a greatest element.
(b) F is a least element.
(c) $\sqcap$ is a greatest lower bound operation.
(d) $\sqcup$ is a least upper bound operation.
(e) $\Rightarrow$ is a relative pseudo-complement operation, i.e. For all $a, b, c \in B$, $c \sqsubseteq a \Rightarrow b$ iff $c \sqcap a \sqsubseteq b$.
(f) For all $a, b \in B$, $(a \Leftrightarrow b) \equiv ((a \Rightarrow b) \sqcap (b \Rightarrow a))$.
(g) For all $a \in B$, $a' \equiv a \Rightarrow F$.
(h) For all $a \in B$, $a'' \equiv a$.

This Boolean prelattice is like a Boolean algebra except that antisymmetry does not hold: two distinct elements can be greater than or equal to each other.

We can now define the class of intensional structures into which FIL is to be interpreted. An *intensional structure* **S** consists of a

[22] We adopt lattice-theoretic symbols that are distinct from those of Section 2.1.1 to highlight the fact that here we have a prelattice with a non-antisymmetric preorder relation.

frame $S = \langle S_A \rangle$, where S_p is a Boolean prelattice, together with enough additional structure to interpret all **FIL** logical constants. The preorder $\sqsubseteq$ is called *entailment*. The specified operations of S_p already provide interpretations for the Boolean logical constants, and the entailment preorder models logical consequence. However, we must add enough operations to interpret (at each type A) the equality and coextensionality predicates as well as the universal and existential quantifiers. The additional operations that we require are as follows.

(102) **Equality:** $=_A$ is interpreted as an *(intensional) identity* operation id_A of type $(p^A)^A$ such that, for all $a, b \in S_A$, $id(a, a) \equiv T$ and $id(a, b) \equiv F$, whenever $a \neq b$.[23]

(103) **Coextensionality:** $\cong_A$ is interpreted as an *extensional identity* operation $extid_A$ of type $(p^A)^A$ such that, for all $a, b \in S_A$, $extid(a, a) \equiv T$, $extid(a, b) \equiv extid(b, a)$, and $(extid(a, b) \sqcap extid(b, c)) \sqsubseteq extid(a, c)$. Also, if $A = C^B$ then for all $f, g \in S_A$, $extid(f, g) \equiv \bigsqcap_{b \in B} extid(f(b), g(b))$. Moreover, $extid_p \equiv \Leftrightarrow$.

(104) **Universal quantification:** $\forall_A$ is interpreted as a *type-restricted universal quantification* operation $\prod_A$ of type p^{p^A} such that, for every $f \in S_{p^A}$, $\prod(f) \equiv \bigsqcap_{a \in A} f(a)$.

(105) **Existential quantification:** $\exists_A$ is interpreted as a *type-restricted existential quantification* operation $\coprod_A$ of type p^{p^A}, such that, for every $f \in S_{p^A}$, $\coprod(f) \equiv \bigsqcup_{a \in A} f(a)$.

Thus universal and existential quantification are treated as infinitary conjunction (greatest lower bound) and disjunction (least upper bound), respectively.

An *intensional model* of **FIL**, is an intensional structure **S**, together with a function *Int* which assigns to each nonlogical constant a type-appropriate intension in S, and to each logical constant the obvious operation in S. If g is an assignment of variables to type-appropriate intensions in S, then *Int* extends uniquely to

23 In this setting, = ($\neq$) is a meta-theoretic notion of identity (non-identity).

an interpretation Int_g of all FIL terms by requiring that $Int_g(x) = g(x)$ for every variable x, and that application and term abstraction receive their customary interpretations; namely, $Int_g(\gamma(\alpha)) = (Int_g(\gamma))(Int_g(\alpha))$, and $Int_g(\lambda x_{\in A}\alpha)$ is the function that maps each $a \in S_A$ to $Int_{g(x/a)}(\alpha)$. Clearly, the value assigned by Int_g to a closed term depends only on Int (not on g), and interpretation respects primitive equality in the sense that λ-equivalent terms, and terms differing only alphabetically in their bound variables, are assigned the same intensions.

To summarize, an intensional model assigns intensions to terms in such a way that logical constants are interpreted as designated operations, term application and abstraction are interpreted in the standard way, and lambda and alphabetic variant-equivalent terms receive the same intensions. Formulas (terms of type p) have as their intensions *propositions* (elements of the Boolean prelattice S_p), terms of type i have as their intensions *individual concepts* (elements of S_i), and A-predicates (terms of type p^A) have as their intensions *A-properties* (propositional functions with domain S_A). Crucially, sentences which are provably co-extensional but not provably equal (λ-interconvertible or alphabetic variant) are interpreted as distinct but equivalent (mutually entailing) propositions.

4.3.2 Constructing Worlds and Denotations Algebraically

Let us hold Int and S fixed. Generalizing Kripke (1959) – and Jonsson and Tarski (1951) – we define a (*possible*) *world* (we have no impossible worlds) to be a maximal consistent sets of propositions, i.e. an ultra filter of the Boolean prelattice S_p. These are in one-to-one correspondence with the *valuations* on S_p, i.e. the Boolean homomorphisms from S_p to the two-element Boolean algebra 2 (or, equivalently, the characteristic functions of ultra filters). The valuation Val_w corresponding to the ultra filter w is w's characteristic function.

Again following Kripke (1959), we define a *modal intensional model* $M = \langle \mathbf{S}, Int, W, R\rangle$, where W is the set of worlds, and R is an accessibility relation on the elements of W. For the present version of FIL we assume that R is an equivalence relation in order to sustain S5.

Given a world w and two intensions s, r of the same type, we say s and r are *w-coextensional* just in case the proposition $extid(s, r)$ is in w. It is easy to see that w-coextensionality is an equivalence relation at each type. We define the type-indexed family $D_w = \langle D_{w,A} \rangle$ of *denotations* at w by type recursion as follows:

(106) (a) $D_{w,p} = 2$ (the truth values, t and f).
(b) $D_{w,i}$ = the quotient of S_i by the w-coextensionality relation (i.e. the individuals are the w-coextensionality equivalence classes of individual concepts).
(c) D_{w,B^A} = the set of functions from S_A to D_B.

For any type A, the denotations of type p^A are functions from S_A to 2, i.e. characteristic functions of sets of A-intensions.

We can extend the valuation Val_w associated with w to all of S (i.e. to intensions of all types) by type recursion.

(107) (a) $Val_w(s) = \mathrm{t}$ if $s \in w$, f otherwise (for s a proposition).
(b) $Val_w(s)$ = the w-coextensionality equivalence class of s, for s an individual concept.
(c) $Val_w(s)$ = the function from S_A to D_B that maps each $a \in S_A$ to $Val_w(s(a))$ (for $s \in S_{B^A}$).

We can prove Thereoms 4 and 5 by type induction.

Theorem 4 *Two intensions are w-coextensional iff they have the same value at w.*

Given a world w and a variable assignment g, we define the *denotation* of a term α at w, relative to g, written $[\![\alpha]\!]_{M,w,g}$, to be $Val_w(Int_g(\alpha))$. If α is closed, the subscript g can be omitted. We then have:

Theorem 5 $[\![\cdot]\!]_{M,w,g}$ *behaves as follows:*

(1) $[\![\alpha]\!]_{M,w,g} = Val_w(Int(\alpha))$, *if α is a constant.*
(2) $[\![\alpha]\!]_{M,w,g} = Val_w(g(\alpha))$, *if α a variable.*
(3) $[\![\gamma(\beta)]\!]_{M,w,g} = [\![\gamma]\!]_{M,w,g}(Int_g(\beta))$.

(4) $[\![\lambda x_{\in A}\beta]\!]_{M,w,g}$ = f, *a function with domain* S_A *such that for any* $a \in S_A$, $f(a) = [\![\beta]\!]_{M,w,g(x/a)}$.
(5) $[\![\top]\!]_{M,w,g}$ = t.
(6) $[\![\bot]\!]_{M,w,g}$ = f.
(7) $[\![\sim\varphi]\!]_{M,w,g}$ = t *iff* $[\![\varphi]\!]_{M,w,g}$ = f.
(8) $[\![\varphi \wedge \psi]\!]_{M,w,g}$ = t *iff* $[\![\varphi]\!]_{M,w,g} = [\![\psi]\!]_{M,w,g}$ = t.
(9) $[\![\varphi \vee \psi]\!]_{M,w,g}$ = t *iff* $[\![\varphi]\!]_{M,w,g}$ = t *or* $[\![\psi]\!]_{M,w,g}$ = t.
(10) $[\![\varphi \to \psi]\!]_{M,w,g}$ = t *iff* $[\![\varphi]\!]_{M,w,g}$ = *f or* $[\![\psi]\!]_{M,w,g}$ = *t*.
(11) $[\![\varphi \leftrightarrow \psi]\!]_{M,w,g}$ = t *iff* $[\![\varphi]\!]_{M,w,g} = [\![\psi]\!]_{M,w,g}$.
(12) $[\![\forall x_{\in A}\varphi]\!]_{M,w,g}$ = t *iff* $[\![\varphi]\!]_{M,w,g(x/a)}$ = t *for all* $a \in S_A$.
(13) $[\![\exists x_{\in A}\varphi]\!]_{M,w,g}$ = t *iff* $[\![\varphi]\!]_{M,w,g(x/a)}$ = t *for some* $a \in S_A$.
(14) $[\![\beta \cong \gamma]\!]_{M,w,g}$ = t *iff* $[\![\beta]\!]_{M,w,g} = [\![\gamma]\!]_{M,w,g}$.
(15) $[\![\beta = \gamma]\!]_{M,w,g}$ = *t iff* $Int_g(\beta) = Int_g(\gamma)$. *(So the truth-value of an equality is independent of the choice of world.)*

In addition to the semantic clauses of Theorem 5 we adopt the following conditions on Val_w.

(108) **Modal Operator Conditions:** For $\varphi_{\in p}$,
(a) $[\![\Box\varphi]\!]_{M,w,g}$ = t iff $[\![\varphi]\!]_{M,w_i,g}$ = t for all $w_i \in W$ such that wRw_i
(b) $[\![\Diamond\varphi]\!]_{M,w,g}$ = t iff $[\![\varphi]\!]_{M,w_i,g}$ = t for some $w_i \in W$ such that wRw_i.

It is not difficult to show that Theorem 6 holds.

Theorem 6 *If there is a proof of a sentence s of FIL, then s is valid relative to the set of models defined for FIL.*

Proof: (Outline) First it is necessary to prove a lemma stating that if there is a model M, a world w_1, and a valuation g such that for the root $1 : s$ of a finished tree Tr, $[\![s]\!]_{M,w_1,g}$ = t, then there is an open path P in Tr in which for every full sentence $\sigma : r$ in P, $[\![r]\!]_{M,w_\sigma,g}$ = t. To establish this lemma, we need to prove the downward correctness of the tableau rules and constraints. This is done by showing that each rule and constraint preserves truth, given the clauses of Theorem 5 and the Modal Operator Conditions (108) of our model theory.

We then prove the lemma through induction on application of the tableau rules and constraints to the sentences in the open path of a tree. The base of the induction is the case in which the tree consists of just one sentence to which no rules or constraints apply. For the inductive step we observe that any expansion P' of an open path P is obtained by a tableau rule to a sentence of P. Downward correctness of the rules ensures that every sentence $\sigma : r$ of P' is true relative to $[\![\cdot]\!]_{M,w_\sigma,g}$, and the sentences of P satisfy the tableau constraints. Hence, at any point in the construction of a finished tree Tr whose root is a sentence $1 : s$ such that $[\![s]\!]_{M,w_1,g} = \text{t}$, there is an open path P in Tr in which for every sentence $\sigma : r$ it is the case that $[\![r]\!]_{M,w_\sigma,g} = \text{t}$. This result holds for both finite and infinite trees (trees with infinite paths). This establishes the lemma.

Given the lemma, it follows that if there is a proof for s, then there is no model M, no world w, and no valuation g such that $[\![\sim s]\!]_{M,w,g} = \text{t}$. Therefore, Theorem 6 holds. □

4.4 Conclusion

We have presented a higher-order fine-grained intensional logic for the semantic representation of natural languages. The logic contains type general predicates for intensional identity and extensional equality. The proof procedure permits us to prove that identity of intension entails identity of extension, but that the converse does not hold. We have constructed an algebraic semantics for our logic relative to which our tableau proof procedure is sound. Unlike alternative hyperintensionalist frameworks that have been proposed, we can distinguish among equivalent propositions without resorting to impossible worlds to sustain the distinction. We treat modality separately from intensions. On our approach, intensions are taken as primary, and truth, denotation, and modality are defined in terms of them.

Chapter 5

Property Theory with Curry Typing

In Chapter 4 we presented a conservative revision of Montague's IL in which we introduced an alternative characterization of intensions while retaining the Church typing and higher-order nature of the system. One of the main reasons for employing higher-order type systems is that they contain functional types, which are required to provide adequate semantic representations for several syntactic categories. A unified treatment of NPs is possible if they are assigned the type of generalized quantifier (functions from properties to propositions, or truth-values). Adjectival and adverbial modifiers correspond to functions from properties to properties (or sets). Sentential modifiers are interpreted as functions from propositions to propositions (truth-values).

As we observed in Chapter 1, IL is developed within an intensional version of Church's (1940) Simple Theory of Types (STT) employing the typed λ-calculus with intension and extension forming operators, and modal operators. Gallin (1975) simplifies this system by replacing the intensional and extensional operators with the basic type s. Barwise and Cooper (1981) invoke a set-theoretic counterpart of STT to develop an account of generalized quantifiers in natural language, and this framework is applied by, among others, Keenan and Stavi (1986), Keenan and Westerståhl (1997), and Lappin (2000a). Cooper (1996) uses a version of the typed λ-calculus to construct a situation theoretic treatment of generalized quantifiers. Groenendijk and Stokhof (1990, 1991) integrate their dynamic logic into a variant of Montague's IL in order to represent certain kinds of discourse anaphora.

In this chapter we propose a more far-reaching departure from MS in which we sustain the radical intensionalist perspective of FIL within a first-order property theory enriched with a flexible Curry type system. We refer to this theory as Property Theory with Curry Typing (PTCT). Like FIL, PTCT permits fine-grained specifications of meaning. Unlike FIL, it is expressed in a first-order framework, and it supports polymorphic, separation, and product types.[24] In developing a radical intensionalist semantics within a first-order framework we are pursuing an approach that bears some connection with ideas suggested by Bealer (1982); Turner (1987, 1992), and Zalta (1988). However, in contrast to this earlier work, PTCT has a robust Curry type system with fully articulated proof and model theories.

Through its use of Curry typing, PTCT contains the full range of functional types. Moreover, it allows for limited (non-iterated) polymorphism, so that it captures the fact that certain natural language expressions, like coordination, correspond to functional types that apply to a variety of distinct argument types. However, quantification in the language of well-formed formulas in PTCT is first-order. Quantification over functional entities and types is expressed through quantification over terms, which are elements of the domain. The model theory is an extension of a standard extensional model for the untyped λ-calculus, with the additional expressive power of Curry types added through a distinct component of the language of terms. The logic remains first-order in character. We prove that the basic PTCT logic (without number theory) is sound and complete.

24 Separation types yield a form of *subtype*.

5.1 PTCT: A Curry-Typed Theory

There are various ways in which we can view PTCT. It can be regarded as a development of PT (Turner 1992) (see Chapter 3). The main difference being that PTCT has a fully-fledged language of types, whereas PT typically mimics types using properties. The addition of types requires changes to the syntax of the language, and the proof theory, in order to give the appropriate behaviour to expressions in which types appear.

These additions ensure that we can represent quantified propositions that explicitly restrict the domain of quantification. For example, if we wish to represent the sentence

(109) John believes everything that Mary believes.

then the quantifier representing *everything* can be restricted to range only over propositions. In PT, such restrictions can only be expressed in the language of wffs.

There are other significant differences. PT has a universal type. It has been argued that this is appropriate for dealing with polymorphic phenomena such as conjunctions, gerunds and infinitives (Chierchia 1984; Chierchia and Turner 1988). However, we find this approach unduly permissive in that it imposes no constraints on the relevant types of the arguments and conjuncts. As we shall see, PTCT can deal with most salient examples using weak polymorphic types. This allows us to impose linguistically motivated constraints on the types of the arguments and conjuncts.

A further distinction is that unlike PT, PTCT does not permit self-application. This constraint is imposed to prevent paradoxes that would otherwise follow from the nature of the type system (in particular, from having a type corresponding to propositions that can appear in terms within the theory).[25]

[25] If a system has an impredicative notion of proposition, and also allows terms involving self-application to form propositions, then it will be inconsistent. PT allows self-application, but has a predicative notion of proposition. Because the type that corresponds to propositions can appear within the terms

PTCT differs from FIL (Chapter 4), and other higher-order logics, in that PTCT effectively adopts a *meta-theoretic* characterization of a semantic theory. Derivations are presented as axioms in a meta-theory, which is folded into the full theory. To convey the basic idea consider that an inference of the form

(110) $a, b \vdash c$

is formulated as something like the axiom

(111) $\mathsf{T}(a) \wedge \mathsf{T}(b) \rightarrow \mathsf{T}(c)$

where $\wedge$ and $\rightarrow$ are meta-level connectives, and $\mathsf{T}(a)$ is a meta-theoretic proposition that asserts that the object level proposition a is true.

Formulating a logic by way of a meta-theory is not novel. See, for example, Turner (1992), Smith (1984), and McCord and Bernth (forthcoming) for instances of this strategy. We have already observed some of the differences between PTCT and the Property Theory of Turner (1992). Smith (1984) indicates how Martin-Löf Type Theory (MLTT) can be interpreted in a Frege Structure in the sense of Aczel (1980). Although Smith internalizes a 'universe' of types, they are precisely the small types of the Frege Structure, which can be internalized in PT. Therefore the limitations of Smith's type system are exactly those of PT, with the additional distinction that Smith is expressing an intuitionistic theory rather than a classical Boolean one. Note that Turner (1992) subsumes Smith (1984).

The meta-theory for PTCT is first-order in character. By giving it an appropriate model, we show that PTCT is a first-order equivalent language.[26]

Our other major departure from more conventional approaches concerns the nature of the types that we incorporate into PTCT. Broadly speaking, types can be either Church-style or Curry-style. In contrast to most typed logics that have been used for

of PTCT, its characterization of propositions is impredicative, so self-application is excluded. This is discussed in more detail in Section 9.4.

[26] This is somewhat akin to giving a Henkin general model for a logic that is expressed in higher-order terms (Henkin 1950).

natural language semantics, PTCT adopts Curry typing for flexibility.

Conceptually, there is a fairly close relationship between the underlying logic captured by the meta-theory of PTCT, and Turner's (1997) IHOL (Intensional Higher Order Logic).

5.2 PTCT: Syntax of the Basic Theory

The core language of PTCT consists of the following sub-languages:

(112) Terms $t ::= x \mid c \mid l \mid T \mid \lambda x(t) \mid (t)t$
(logical constants) $l ::= \hat{\sim} \mid \hat{\wedge} \mid \hat{\vee} \mid \hat{\rightarrow} \mid \hat{\leftrightarrow} \mid \hat{\forall} \mid \hat{\exists} \mid \hat{=}_T \mid \hat{\cong}_T \mid \epsilon T$

(113) Types $T ::= B \mid \mathsf{Prop} \mid T \Longrightarrow T'$

(114) Wffs $\varphi ::= \alpha \mid {\sim}\varphi \mid (\varphi \wedge \varphi') \mid (\varphi \vee \varphi') \mid (\varphi \rightarrow \varphi')$
$\mid (\varphi \leftrightarrow \varphi') \mid (\forall x \varphi) \mid (\exists x \varphi)$
atomic wff $\alpha ::= (t =_T s) \mid t \in T \mid t \cong_T s \mid {}^{\mathsf{T}}t$

The language of terms is the untyped λ-calculus, enriched with constants c, and logical constants l. Types T are also terms.[27] The presence of constants c allows us to introduce additional λ-calculus terms in subsequent discussions without always being obliged to give an encoding of the new notion in pure (i.e. constant-free) λ-calculus.

The language of types contains the basic type of individuals B, propositions Prop, and general function space types $T \Longrightarrow T'$.

The language of wffs is a first-order language together with type judgements $t \in T$, typed identity $=_T$ (intensional equality) and equivalence $\cong_T$ (extensional equality), and truth judgments ${}^{\mathsf{T}}t$.

[27] It is possible to consider reformulating the theory using a typed λ-calculus with abstraction of the form $\lambda x_{\in T}(t)$. Separation types, which are introduced later, could then be treated directly as sugar for a typed λ-abstract.

In the case of the untyped calculus used here, it is reasonable to consider adding untyped λ-identity as an atomic wff $(t =_\lambda t)$, rather than adding the usual α, β, η rules as substitution rules in the tableau rules for the system.

In principle at least, the latter can apply to all terms t, but it only makes sense to apply it to terms that are intended to represent propositions (that is, $t \in$ Prop). To do otherwise would be to entertain a category mistake.

The language of terms is used to *represent* the interpretations of natural language expressions. It has no internal logic. By this, we mean that it is not possible to perform inferences *directly* with term representations of propositions. Inferences are concerned with establishing relationships between the truth conditions of propositions and terms representing propositions. In the case of PTCT, such relationships are expressed in the language of wffs, which acts as a *meta-language* for the language of terms.

With an appropriate proof theory, the simple language of types together with the language of terms can be combined to produce a Curry-typed λ-calculus. The first-order language of wffs is used to formulate type judgements for terms, and truth conditions for those terms judged to be in Prop.

It is important to distinguish between the notion of a proposition itself (in the language of wff), and that of a term that *represents* a proposition (in the language of terms). $^{\mathsf{T}}(t)$ will be a true wff whenever the proposition represented by the term t is true, and a false wff whenever the proposition represented by t is false. The representation of a proposition t ($\in$ Prop) is distinct from its truth conditions ($^{\mathsf{T}}(t)$). This distinction permits us to identify the intension of an expression with its term representation, and so to distinguish between provably equivalent terms. Specifically, in PTCT distinct propositional terms can have the same truth conditions.

Later, in Section 5.5, we will consider some extensions to the theory.

5.3 A Proof Theory for PTCT

We construct a tableau proof theory for PTCT.[28] Its rules can be broken down into the following kinds.

[28] For an introduction to tableau proof procedures for first-order logic with identity, see Jeffrey (1982), based on work by Beth (1956) and Smullyan (1968).

- The basic connectives of the wff: These have the standard classical first-order behaviour.
- Identity of terms ($=_T$): These are the usual rules of the untyped λ-calculus with α, β and η reduction, with the constraint that the related terms are known to be of the same type.
- Typing of λ-terms: These are essentially the rules of the Curry-typed calculus, augmented with rules governing those terms that represent propositions (Prop).
- Truth conditions for propositions: Additional rules for the language of wffs that govern the truth conditions of terms in Prop (which represent propositions).
- Equivalence ($\cong_T$): The theory has an internal notion of extensional equivalence which is given the expected behaviour.

Below we present the tableau rules for PTCT. The symbol * indicates that the corresponding proposition has been used, and does not need to be considered again.

5.3.1 General Rule Forms

The four general kinds of rules, *A*, *B*, *C*, and *D* (see Section 4.2.2) are repeated here.

***A*-Rule**

A^*

A_1
A_2

***B*-Rule**

B^*

$B_1 \quad B_2$

***C*(*d*)-Rule**

C

$C[d/x]$

where d occurs on the path (or is the only constant occurring in the path), and d, x are of the same type

***D*(*d*)-Rule**

D^*

$D[d/x]$

where d does not occur previously on the path, and d, x are of the same type

As usual, there are also *closure rules* which indicate when a path is closed due to a contradiction. Partly due to the typing system, and partly to simplify the proof of completeness, additional closure rules are given in addition to the usual rule that states that a path is closed if it contains the formulae A and $\sim A$ for any proposition A. Rules that require two premises are represented as single premise rules with a side-condition.

The specific rules for wffs (the core classical logic, λ-equivalence, equivalence and identity), types and propositions are detailed next.

5.3.2 Rules for Wffs

Classical Rules
The following rules are standard, as we adopt the usual rules for the core logic of wff.

***A*-Rules**

Conjunction

$$\begin{array}{c} (\varphi \wedge \psi)* \\ | \\ \varphi \\ \psi \end{array}$$

Bi-implication

$$\begin{array}{c} (\varphi \leftrightarrow \psi)* \\ | \\ (\varphi \rightarrow \psi) \\ (\psi \rightarrow \varphi) \end{array}$$

Disjunction′

$$\begin{array}{c} \sim(\varphi \vee \psi)* \\ | \\ \sim\varphi \\ \sim\psi \end{array}$$

Implication′

$$\begin{array}{c} \sim(\varphi \rightarrow \psi)* \\ | \\ \varphi \\ \sim\psi \end{array}$$

Double Negation

$$\begin{array}{c} \sim\sim\varphi* \\ | \\ \varphi \end{array}$$

B-**Rules**

Disjunction

$$(\varphi \vee \psi)*$$

φ | ψ

Conjunction′

$$\sim(\varphi \wedge \psi)*$$

$\sim\varphi$ | $\sim\psi$

Implication

$$(\varphi \rightarrow \psi)*$$

$\sim\varphi$ | ψ

Bi-implication′

$$\sim(\varphi \leftrightarrow \psi)*$$

$\sim(\varphi \rightarrow \psi)$ | $\sim(\psi \rightarrow \varphi)$

C-**Rules**

∀ Quantification

$$\forall x\varphi$$

$$\varphi[d/x]$$

∃ Quantification′

$$\sim\exists x\varphi$$

$$\sim\varphi[d/x]$$

D-**Rules**

∃ Quantification

$$\exists x\varphi*$$

$$\varphi[d/x]$$

∀ Quantification′

$$\sim\forall x\varphi*$$

$$\sim\varphi[d/x]$$

⊥-**Rules**

Path closure can be derived under the following circumstances.

Contradiction (1)
φ closes a branch if $\sim\varphi$

Contradiction (2)
$\sim\varphi$ closes a branch if φ

Now that we have the standard rules in place, we can consider the rules for substituting λ-equivalent terms, and, subsequently, the rules that govern the PTCT notions of equivalence and identity.

λ-Rules

The following equivalence and identity rules implement the usual α, β, and η rules of the λ-calculus as substitution rules.

A-**Rules**

β-reduction

$$\frac{\ldots(\lambda ut)(a)\ldots}{\ldots t[a/u]\ldots} \quad \textit{a not bound in t}$$

η-reduction

$$\frac{\ldots\lambda u(tu)\ldots}{\ldots t\ldots} \quad \textit{u not free in t}$$

C-**Rules**

α-reduction

$$\frac{\ldots\lambda xt\ldots}{\ldots\lambda d(t[d/x])\ldots} \quad \textit{d not free in t, and d, x are of the same type}$$

The following equivalence and identity rules are intended to give the appropriate logical behaviour to statements of equivalence in the language of wffs.

A-**Rules**

Substitution

$$\frac{\varphi}{\varphi[t/s]} \quad t =_T s \text{ or } s =_T t$$

Identity

$$\frac{t \in T}{t =_T t}$$

Equivalence (1) – reflexivity

$$t \in T$$
$$|$$
$$t \cong_T t$$

Equivalence (2) – symmetry

$$t \cong_T s \qquad t, s \in T$$
$$|$$
$$s \cong_T t$$

Equivalence (3) – transitivity

$$t \cong_T s \qquad t, s, u \in T; s \cong_T u$$
$$|$$
$$t \cong_T u$$

Equivalence (4) – in Prop

$$t \cong_{\mathsf{Prop}} s$$
$$|$$
$$^{\mathsf{T}}t \leftrightarrow {}^{\mathsf{T}}s$$

Equivalence′ (5) – in Prop

$$\sim(t \cong_{\mathsf{Prop}} s)$$
$$|$$
$$\sim(^{\mathsf{T}}t \leftrightarrow {}^{\mathsf{T}}s)$$

***C*-Rules**

Co-extensionality (1)

$$s \cong_{(S \Longrightarrow T)} t \qquad d \in S; \; t, s \in (S \Longrightarrow T)$$
$$|$$
$$s(d) \cong_T t(d)$$

***D*-Rules**

Co-extensionality′ (2)

$$\sim(s \cong_{(S \Longrightarrow T)} t) \qquad d \in S; \; t, s \in (S \Longrightarrow T)$$
$$|$$
$$\sim(s(d) \cong_T t(d))$$

⊥-Rules

Path closure can be derived under the following circumstances:

Equivalence within a Type

$t \cong_T t'$ closes a branch if $t \notin T$

Identity within a Type

$(t =_T t')$ closes a branch if $t \notin T$

5.3.3 Type Inference Rules

These rules govern the inference of type membership of terms in the language of wffs.

A-Rules

General Function Spaces (1)

$$\begin{array}{c} t \in (S \Longrightarrow T) \\ | \\ \forall x(x \in S \rightarrow tx \in T) \end{array}$$

General Function Spaces (2)

$$\begin{array}{c} t \notin (S \Longrightarrow T) \\ | \\ \exists x(x \in S \wedge tx \notin T) \end{array}$$

Negated Propositions

$$\begin{array}{c} \hat{\sim} t \notin \mathsf{Prop} \\ | \\ t \notin \mathsf{Prop} \end{array}$$

Universal Propositions

$$\begin{array}{c} (\hat{\forall} x \epsilon S(t)) \notin \mathsf{Prop} \\ | \\ (\lambda x t) \notin (S \Longrightarrow \mathsf{Prop}) \end{array}$$

Existential Propositions

$$\begin{array}{c} (\hat{\exists} x \epsilon S(t)) \notin \mathsf{Prop} \\ | \\ (\lambda x t) \notin (S \Longrightarrow \mathsf{Prop}) \end{array}$$

Equivalence

$$\begin{array}{cc} t \in T & t' \in T \\ | & \\ (t \hat{\cong}_T t') \in \mathsf{Prop} & \end{array}$$

Identity

$$\begin{array}{cc} t \in T & t' \in T \\ | & \\ (t \hat{=}_T t') \subset \mathsf{Prop} & \end{array}$$

B-Rules

Conjunctive Propositions

$$\begin{array}{c} (t \mathbin{\hat{\wedge}} t') \notin \mathsf{Prop} \\ \diagup \quad \diagdown \\ t \notin \mathsf{Prop} \qquad t' \notin \mathsf{Prop} \end{array}$$

Disjunctive Propositions

$$\begin{array}{c} (t \mathbin{\hat{\vee}} t') \notin \mathsf{Prop} \\ \diagup \quad \diagdown \\ t \notin \mathsf{Prop} \qquad t' \notin \mathsf{Prop} \end{array}$$

Implicative Propositions

$$\begin{array}{c} (t \mathbin{\hat{\rightarrow}} t') \notin \mathsf{Prop} \\ \diagup \quad \diagdown \\ t \notin \mathsf{Prop} \qquad t' \notin \mathsf{Prop} \end{array}$$

Bi-implicative Propositions

$$\begin{array}{c} (t \mathbin{\hat{\leftrightarrow}} t') \notin \mathsf{Prop} \\ \diagup \quad \diagdown \\ t \notin \mathsf{Prop} \qquad t' \notin \mathsf{Prop} \end{array}$$

⊥-Rules

True Propositions

${}^{\mathsf{T}}s$ closes a branch if $s \notin \mathsf{Prop}$

5.3.4 Truth Rules

The following rules effectively encode the truth conditions of terms that represent propositions.

***A*-Rules**

Negation

$$\begin{array}{ll} {}^{\mathsf{T}}(\hat{\sim} s)* & s \in \mathsf{Prop} \\ \quad | & \\ \sim {}^{\mathsf{T}}s & \end{array}$$

Conjunction

$$\begin{array}{ll} {}^{\mathsf{T}}(s \mathbin{\hat{\wedge}} t)* & s,t \in \mathsf{Prop} \\ \quad | & \\ {}^{\mathsf{T}}s \wedge {}^{\mathsf{T}}t & \end{array}$$

Disjunction

$$\begin{array}{ll} {}^{\mathsf{T}}(s \mathbin{\hat{\vee}} t)* & s,t \in \mathsf{Prop} \\ \quad | & \\ {}^{\mathsf{T}}s \vee {}^{\mathsf{T}}t & \end{array}$$

Implication

$$\begin{array}{ll} {}^{\mathsf{T}}(s \mathbin{\hat{\rightarrow}} t)* & s,t \in \mathsf{Prop} \\ \quad | & \\ {}^{\mathsf{T}}s \rightarrow {}^{\mathsf{T}}t & \end{array}$$

Bi-implication

$$\begin{array}{ll} {}^{\mathsf{T}}(s \mathbin{\hat{\leftrightarrow}} t)* & s,t \in \mathsf{Prop} \\ \quad | & \\ {}^{\mathsf{T}}s \leftrightarrow {}^{\mathsf{T}}t & \end{array}$$

∀ Quantification

$$\begin{array}{ll} {}^{\mathsf{T}}(\hat{\forall} x \epsilon S(t))* & (\lambda xt) \in (S \Longrightarrow \mathsf{Prop}) \\ \quad | & \\ \forall x(x \in S \rightarrow {}^{\mathsf{T}}t) & \end{array}$$

∃ Quantification

$$^{\mathsf{T}}(\hat{\exists} x \epsilon S(t))* \quad (\lambda xt) \in (S \Longrightarrow \mathsf{Prop})$$
$$\exists x(x \in S \wedge {}^{\mathsf{T}}t)$$

Equivalence

$$^{\mathsf{T}}(s \mathrel{\hat{\cong}_T} t)* \quad s,t \in T$$
$$(s \cong_T t)$$

Identity

$$^{\mathsf{T}}(s \mathrel{\hat{=}_T} t)* \quad s,t \in T$$
$$(s =_T t)$$

Negation′

$$\sim {}^{\mathsf{T}}(\hat{\sim} s)* \quad s \in \mathsf{Prop}$$
$$^{\mathsf{T}}s$$

Conjunction′

$$\sim {}^{\mathsf{T}}(s \mathbin{\hat{\wedge}} t)* \quad s,t \in \mathsf{Prop}$$
$$\sim({}^{\mathsf{T}}s \wedge {}^{\mathsf{T}}t)$$

Disjunction′

$$\sim {}^{\mathsf{T}}(s \mathbin{\hat{\vee}} t)* \quad s,t \in \mathsf{Prop}$$
$$\sim({}^{\mathsf{T}}s \vee {}^{\mathsf{T}}t)$$

Implication′

$$\sim {}^{\mathsf{T}}(s \mathbin{\hat{\rightarrow}} t)* \quad s,t \in \mathsf{Prop}$$
$$\sim({}^{\mathsf{T}}s \rightarrow {}^{\mathsf{T}}t)$$

Bi-implication′

$$\sim {}^{\mathsf{T}}(s \mathbin{\hat{\leftrightarrow}} t)* \quad s,t \in \mathsf{Prop}$$
$$\sim({}^{\mathsf{T}}s \leftrightarrow {}^{\mathsf{T}}t)$$

∀ Quantification′

$$\sim {}^{\mathsf{T}}(\hat{\forall} x \epsilon S(t))* \quad (\lambda xt) \in (S \Longrightarrow \mathsf{Prop})$$
$$\sim \forall x(x \in S \rightarrow {}^{\mathsf{T}}t)$$

∃ Quantification′

$$\sim {}^{\mathsf{T}}(\hat{\exists} x \epsilon S(t))* \quad (\lambda xt) \in (S \Longrightarrow \mathsf{Prop})$$
$$\sim \exists x(x \in S \wedge {}^{\mathsf{T}}t)$$

Equivalence′

$$\sim {}^{\mathsf{T}}(s \mathrel{\hat{\cong}_T} t)* \quad s,t \in T$$
$$\sim(s \cong_T t)$$

Identity′

$$\sim {}^{\mathsf{T}}(s \mathrel{\hat{=}_T} t)* \quad s,t \in T$$
$$\sim(s =_T t)$$

5.4 Example Proof

In Figure 5.1, we give an example of a proof using this tableau system. The example represents an agent's beliefs about another agent's beliefs, where the object of the first agent's belief is a term

1 $\mathrm{bel}'_e \in (\mathrm{Prop} \Longrightarrow \mathrm{Prop})$

2 $\mathrm{bel}'_d \in (\mathrm{Prop} \Longrightarrow \mathrm{Prop})$

3 $\varphi \in \mathrm{Prop}$

4 $\mathrm{bel}'_e(\hat{\forall} x \epsilon \mathrm{Prop}(\mathrm{bel}'_d(x) \mathrel{\hat{\rightarrow}} \varphi)) \notin \mathrm{Prop}$

5 $\forall x(x \in \mathrm{Prop} \rightarrow \mathrm{bel}'_e(x) \in \mathrm{Prop})$

6 $(\hat{\forall} x \epsilon \mathrm{Prop}(\mathrm{bel}'_d(x) \mathrel{\hat{\rightarrow}} \varphi)) \in \mathrm{Prop} \rightarrow \mathrm{bel}'_e(\hat{\forall} x \epsilon \mathrm{Prop}(\mathrm{bel}'_d(x) \mathrel{\hat{\rightarrow}} \varphi)) \in \mathrm{Prop}$

7 $(\hat{\forall} x \epsilon \mathrm{Prop}(\mathrm{bel}'_d(x) \mathrel{\hat{\rightarrow}} \varphi)) \notin \mathrm{Prop}$; $\underline{\mathrm{bel}'_e(\hat{\forall} x \epsilon \mathrm{Prop}(\mathrm{bel}'_d(x) \mathrel{\hat{\rightarrow}} \varphi)) \in \mathrm{Prop}}$

8 $\lambda x(\mathrm{bel}'_d(x) \mathrel{\hat{\rightarrow}} \varphi) \notin (\mathrm{Prop} \Longrightarrow \mathrm{Prop})$

9 $\exists y(y \in \mathrm{Prop} \wedge \lambda x(\mathrm{bel}'_d(x) \mathrel{\hat{\rightarrow}} \varphi)(y) \notin \mathrm{Prop})$

10 $\exists y(y \in \mathrm{Prop} \wedge (\mathrm{bel}'_d(y) \mathrel{\hat{\rightarrow}} \varphi) \notin \mathrm{Prop})$

11 $a \in \mathrm{Prop} \wedge (\mathrm{bel}'_d(a) \mathrel{\hat{\rightarrow}} \varphi) \notin \mathrm{Prop}$

12 $a \in \mathrm{Prop}$

13 $(\mathrm{bel}'_d(a) \mathrel{\hat{\rightarrow}} \varphi) \notin \mathrm{Prop}$

14 $\mathrm{bel}'_d(a) \notin \mathrm{Prop}$; $\underline{\varphi \notin \mathrm{Prop}}$

15 $a \in \mathrm{Prop} \rightarrow \mathrm{bel}'_d(a) \in \mathrm{Prop}$

16 $\underline{a \notin \mathrm{Prop}}$; $\underline{\mathrm{bel}'_d(a) \in \mathrm{Prop}}$

FIGURE 5.1 Example proof

Note: Lines 1, 2, 3 are premises. 4 is the negated conclusion. 5 follows from 1 (General Function Spaces). The RHS of 7 contradicts 4. 9 uses Negated General Function Spaces. 10 uses β-reduction. The RHS of 14 contradicts 3. 15 is an instantiation of 5. RHS of 16 contradicts 14. LHS of 16 contradicts 12.

corresponding to a proposition. Let bel'_e be a function from Prop to Prop that represents the relation *e believes that*, where e is an agent of belief, and similarly for bel'_d. Let φ be a proposition. Take p to be the term representing the proposition *for every proposition x, if d believes x, then* φ. We prove that these assumptions entail that *e believes that* p is proposition.

Specifically, we show that

(115) $\mathsf{bel}'_e(\hat{\forall} x \epsilon \mathsf{Prop}(\mathsf{bel}'_d(x) \hat{\rightarrow} \varphi)) \in \mathsf{Prop}$

follows from

(116) $\mathsf{bel}'_e \in (\mathsf{Prop} \Longrightarrow \mathsf{Prop})$
$\mathsf{bel}'_d \in (\mathsf{Prop} \Longrightarrow \mathsf{Prop})$
$\varphi \in \mathsf{Prop}$

using the tableau rules given above.

Proofs concerning a term's type are important, as we need to be able to show that a term represents a proposition before we can reason with its truth conditions.

5.5 Extending the Type System

What we have presented so far is a highly intensional formal logic with a simple type system, expressed in a Curry-style. While this type system may be sufficient to deal with core issues in natural language semantics, there are cases where a richer type system is required. Here we consider some possible extensions that are motivated by the concerns of natural language semantics.

5.5.1 A Universal Type

One possible extension that we could consider is to add a universal type Δ, and rules corresponding to the following axiom:

(117) UT: $x \in \Delta \leftrightarrow x = x$

One reason for adopting such an extension is that it would make it possible to apply Chierchia's analysis of nominalization (Chierchia 1982) directly within PTCT (see Section 3.4.3). For example, phrases such as *is fun* can take nouns, gerunds and infinitives as arguments, as in:

(118) (a) Tennis is fun.
(b) Playing tennis is fun.
(c) To play tennis is fun.

The last two sentences are examples of nominalization; gerund and infinitive verbs can function as nouns in role of sentential subject. Chierchia accounts for this by arguing that such phrases should be represented as functions that take arguments of any type to yield a proposition. That is, they have the type $\Delta \Longrightarrow \mathsf{Prop}$.[29]

As Chierchia observes, the universal type also allows for an analysis of natural language conjunction. Conjunctions such as *and* and *or* can generate coordinate structures over a variety of syntact categories (and corresponding semantic types). We can capture this type generality of coordination by assigning it the type $\Delta \Longrightarrow (\Delta \Longrightarrow \Delta)$.

Unfortunately this extension is inconsistent in PTCT if Prop is a type, as it is in our proposed formulation. To see this, consider the term rr, where $r = \lambda x \hat{\exists} y \epsilon (\Delta \Longrightarrow \mathsf{Prop})(x \hat{=}_{\Delta \Longrightarrow \mathsf{Prop}} y \mathbin{\hat{\wedge}} \hat{\sim} xy)$.

Although Chierchia's solution for dealing with gerunds and infinitives is not available to us in PTCT, there are other consistent extensions that we can adopt. One of these, a restricted polymorphism (Section 5.5.4), provides an alternative means of addressing the nominalization examples, and a more precise way of handling the typing of natural language coordination.

First, we turn to several other types, one of which we will exploit extensively in our analysis of natural language anaphora (Chapter 7), and another in our accounts of ellipsis resolution (Chapter 7) and of underspecified scope resolution (Chapter 8).

29 According to Chierchia, this approach also allows us to account for cases of apparent self-predication, as in *Fun is fun*.

5.5.2 Separation Types

Separation types are a variety of subtype. They are expressed in the form $\{x \in T : \varphi\}$, for some T and φ. An element is of this type if it is a term of type T for which the proposition φ is true when the term is substituted for x in φ. The reason that we consider separation types here is that they will be exploited in Chapter 7, which adopts a proposal for the semantic representation of quantifiers suggested by Lappin (1989), and Lappin and Francez (1994).

To add separation types to **PTCT**, we add $\{x \in T : \varphi'\}$ to the types, and a tableau rule that implements the following axiom:

(119) SP: $z \in \{x \in T.\varphi'\} \leftrightarrow (z \in T \wedge \varphi'[z/x])$

That is:

Separation Types

$z \in \{x \in T.\varphi'\}^*$

$z \in T$
$\varphi'[z/x]$

Negated Separation Types

$z \notin \{x \in T.\varphi'\}^*$

$z \notin T$ | $\sim \varphi'[z/x]$

where $\notin$ has its usual intended meaning

There is an important issue here concerning the nature of φ. To help ensure the theory is first-order in character, this type needs to be term representable, so φ' must be term representable. To this end, we can define a term representable fragment of the language of wffs. First, we introduce syntactic sugar for typed quantification in the wffs.

(120) (a) $\forall_T x\varphi =_{\mathsf{def}} \forall x(x \in T \rightarrow \varphi)$
(b) $\exists_T x\varphi =_{\mathsf{def}} \exists x(x \in T \wedge \varphi)$

Wffs with these typed quantifiers, and without free-floating type judgements, will then have direct intensional analogues – that is, term representations – which will always be propositions. We can define representable wffs by φ':

(121) $\varphi' ::= \alpha' \mid (\sim\varphi') \mid (\varphi' \wedge \psi') \mid (\varphi' \vee \psi') \mid (\varphi' \rightarrow \psi') \mid$
$(\varphi' \leftrightarrow \psi') \mid (\forall_T x \varphi') \mid (\exists_T x \varphi')$
(atomic representable wffs) $\alpha' ::= (t =_T s) \mid t \cong_T s \mid {}^{\mathsf{T}}t$

The term representations $\ulcorner\varphi'\urcorner$ of representable wffs φ' are given by the following recursive definition:

(122) (a) $\ulcorner\sim a\urcorner = \hat{\sim}\ulcorner a\urcorner$
(b) $\ulcorner a \wedge b\urcorner = \ulcorner a\urcorner \mathbin{\hat{\wedge}} \ulcorner b\urcorner$
(c) $\ulcorner a \vee b\urcorner = \ulcorner a\urcorner \mathbin{\hat{\vee}} \ulcorner b\urcorner$
(d) $\ulcorner a \rightarrow b\urcorner = \ulcorner a\urcorner \mathbin{\hat{\rightarrow}} \ulcorner b\urcorner$
(e) $\ulcorner a \leftrightarrow b\urcorner = \ulcorner a\urcorner \mathbin{\hat{\leftrightarrow}} \ulcorner b\urcorner$
(f) $\ulcorner a \cong_T b\urcorner = a \mathbin{\hat{\cong}_T} b$
(g) $\ulcorner a =_T b\urcorner = a \mathbin{\hat{=}_T} b$
(h) $\ulcorner {}^{\mathsf{T}}t\urcorner = t$
(i) $\ulcorner \forall_T x.a\urcorner = \hat{\forall} x \epsilon T \ulcorner a\urcorner$
(j) $\ulcorner \exists_T x.a\urcorner = \hat{\exists} x \epsilon T \ulcorner a\urcorner$

The following theorem is an immediate consequence of the recursive definition of representable wffs and their term representations:

Theorem 7 (Representability) $\ulcorner\varphi'\urcorner \in \mathsf{Prop}$ *for all representable wffs* φ'*, and furthermore* ${}^{\mathsf{T}}\ulcorner\varphi'\urcorner \leftrightarrow \varphi'$*.*

5.5.3 Comprehension Types

For completeness, we can consider comprehension types. These are types defined in terms of a proposition. They are usually written in the form $\{x : \varphi\}$. Elements are of this type if the proposition φ is true when the element is substituted for x in φ.

Usually comprehension can be derived from SP and UT. We are forgoing UT to avoid paradoxes (Section 5.5.1), so we have to define comprehension independently. The same arguments apply as for SP concerning representability.

We add the type $\{x : \varphi'\}$ and a tableau rule corresponding to the following axiom:

(123) COMP: $z \in \{x : \varphi\} \leftrightarrow \varphi[z/x]$

The effect of this axiom can be achieved by the following tableau rules:

Comprehension Types	**Negated Comprehension Types**	
$z \in \{x : \varphi'\}^*$	$z \notin \{x : \varphi'\}^*$	*where $\notin$ has its usual intended meaning*
$\mid$	$\mid$	
$\varphi'[z/x]$	$\sim \varphi'[z/x]$	

Given that COMP = SP + UT, where UT is the Universal Type $\Delta = \{x : x \mathrel{\hat{=}} x\}$, we would derive a paradox if $=$ was not typed. This is because in PTCT Prop is a type. So rr, where $r = \lambda x \hat{\exists} y \in (\Delta \Longrightarrow \mathsf{Prop})[x \mathrel{\hat{=}} y \mathbin{\hat{\wedge}} \hat{\sim} xy]$ produces a paradoxical propositional. Our use of a typed intensional identity predicate filters out the paradox because it must be possible to prove that the two expressions for which $=_T$ is asserted are of type T independently of the identity assertion. $s =_T t$ iff $s, t \in T$ and $s = t$.

5.5.4 Polymorphic Types

As we have observed, natural language exhibits flexibility in the categories to which different syntactic elements can belong. Chierchia's examples of nominalization, and natural language coordination, discussed in Section 5.5.1, illustrate this phenomena.

In formal systems, this kind of behaviour is generally characterized by *polymorphism*. Here we formalize a particular kind of polymorphism in PTCT, and indicate how it can address at least some of the data for which a universal type has been proposed.

There are many varieties of polymorphism, including schematic polymorphism, implicit polymorphism, explicit polymorphism, and impredicative polymorphism.

Schematic polymorphism is a syntatic device whereby a metatheoretic symbol is used to abbreviate a range of types. Such symbols are, effectively, syntactic sugar for a disjunction of expressions in which the schematic types are consistently replaced by ground types.

The other forms of polymorphism are genuine extensions to the type system, and require the addition of type variables. In the case of implicit polymorphism, the type variables are universally quantified. It is this kind of polymorphism that we shall formulate here.

With explicit polymorphism, relations and functions in effect contain type variables that can be instantiated by arguments. As we will see in Chapter 8, it might turn out this is actually a more appropriate form of polymorphism for theories of natural language semantics.

Impredicative polymorphism is a particularly powerful device, which is discussed below. It appears that this power is neither required, nor appropriate, for natural language semantics.

To adopt implicit polymorphic types within PTCT, we enrich the language of types to include type variables X, and the wffs to include quantification over types $\forall X\varphi, \exists X\varphi$. We add the following tableau rules:

Universal Type-Quantification

$\forall X\varphi$
|
$\varphi[K/X]$

where K is a type that occurs on the path (or is the only type occurring in the path)

Existential Type-Quantification

$\exists X\varphi^*$
|
$\varphi[K/X]$

where type K does not occur on the path

Negated Type-Quantification

$\sim QX\varphi^*$
|
$Q'X \sim \varphi$

where Q′ is the dual of Q

We add $\Pi X.T$ to the language of types, governed by the tableau rule corresponding to the following axiom:

(124) PM: $f \in \Pi X.T \leftrightarrow \forall X(f \in T)$

The effect of this axiom can be achieved by the following tableau rules:

Polymorphic Types	**Negated Polymorphic Types**	
$f \in \Pi X.T^*$	$f \notin \Pi X.T^*$	*where $\notin$ has its usual intended meaning*
$\vert$	$\vert$	
$\forall X(f \in T)$	$\exists X(f \notin T)$	

Polymorphic types permit us to accommodate the fact that natural language expressions such as coordination and certain verbs can apply as functions to arguments of different types. In particular, we can account for the data given in Section 5.5.1. In the case of the nominalization facts of Chierchia (1982) given in (118) on page 86, we take *is fun* to be of type $\Pi X.X \Longrightarrow \mathsf{Prop}$. Conjunctions, such as *and*, which can combine categories of any type to give an expression of the same type, are of the type $\Pi X.X \Longrightarrow (X \Longrightarrow X)$.[30]

PM is impredicative, i.e. the type quantification ranges over the types that are being defined. Impredicativity greatly increases the power of the language, which is problematic if we wish to sustain a recursively enumerable theory. It can also lead to paradoxes under certain conditions. To avoid these difficulties, we adopt a restricted form of polymorphism.

(125) PM′: $f \in \Pi X.T \leftrightarrow \forall X(f \in T)$ where X ranges only over non-polymorphic types.

This constraint limits quantification over types to type variables that take non-polymorphic types as values. Therefore, we rule out iterated type polymorphism in which polymorphic functions can apply to polymorphic arguments. This weak version of polymorphism seems entirely adequate to express the instances of multiple type assignment that occur in natural languages (van Benthem 1991). The tableau rules do not need to be changed to incorporate PM′, provided that only non-polymorphic types are substituted for type variables in the rules for type quantification.

[30] This does not immediately account for Chierchia's example of apparent self-predication 'Fun is fun.' Nor does it deal with alleged cases of cross-categorial conjunction (Gazdar 1980; Sag 2003).

Even predicative, implicit polymorphism may not be a perfect match for natural language polymorphism. *Explicit* polymorphism may be more appropriate if we wish to deal elegantly with the fact that generalized quantifiers appear to be able to range over different types. It seems natural to say that the noun phrase *every belief* denotes a set (property) of properties of propositions, whereas *every book* denotes a set (property) of properties of individuals. The type of the determiner *every* is then determined by the type of its argument (*book* and *belief* in these examples). This kind of constraint is expressible with explicit polymorphic types. The determiner *every* would then have an argument position that can be supplied by the type of the noun with which it combines. We leave the modification of PTCT from implicit to explicit polymorphic types as an exercise for the interested reader.

5.5.5 Product Types

Product types of the form $S \otimes T$ are useful if we wish to allow functional terms to accept more than one argument at a time. Elements of such a type are pairs of terms, where the first element of the pair is in S, and the second is in T. This type is different in kind from the other types presented so far in that it imposes a structural constraint on its elements: they must be pairs. λ-calculus allows us to define the required notions of pairs and terms, as in PT (Section 3.4).

(126)
$$\langle x, y\rangle =_{\text{def}} \lambda z(z(x)(y))$$
$$\text{fst} =_{\text{def}} \lambda p(p\lambda xy(x))$$
$$\text{snd} =_{\text{def}} \lambda p(p\lambda xy(y))$$

Pairs can be nested, and product type formation can be iterated. This allows arbitrary finite product types to be defined.

Product types are used in Chapter 7 and Chapter 8. In the former case, they help express the treatment of ellipsis. For this application, they may be dispensible. The operations of currying and uncurrying show how it is possible to establish an encoding and decoding relationship between a function of type $\langle T, T'\rangle \Longrightarrow T''$ and a function of type $T \Longrightarrow (T' \Longrightarrow T'')$, for example. A form of currying could be applied to eliminate the product types in the treatment of ellipsis, although the theory would not then be expressed in the most natural terms.

In the case of Chapter 8, product types are used to specify data-structures that are invoked in a treatment of underspecification. These data-structures are intended to behave like lists. However, in constrast to the more usual homogeneously typed lists, their elements may be of different types. This property is exploited in the treatment of underspecification given in Chapter 8 to allow scope neutral representations of sentences involving generalized quantification of different types.

To incorporate product types in PTCT, we add the type $S \otimes T$, and a tableau rule corresponding to the following axiom:

(127) PROD: $\langle x, y\rangle \in (S \otimes T) \leftrightarrow x \in S \wedge y \in T$

The effect of this axiom can be achieved by the following tableau rules:

Product Types

$\langle x, y\rangle \in (S \otimes T)^*$

$x \in S$

$y \in T$

Negated Product Types

$\langle x, y\rangle \notin (S \otimes T)^*$

$x \notin S$ $\quad$ $y \notin T$

where $\notin$ *has its usual intended meaning*

5.5.6 Final Syntax

Adopting the extensions discussed above, which are constrained to prevent the generation of paradoxes, we arrive at the following syntax for PTCT:

(128) (logical constants)	l	::=	$\hat{\sim} \mid \hat{\wedge} \mid \hat{\vee} \mid \hat{\rightarrow} \mid \hat{\leftrightarrow} \mid \hat{\forall} \mid \hat{\exists} \mid \hat{=}_T \mid \hat{\cong}_T \mid \epsilon T$
(terms)	t	::=	$x \mid c \mid l \mid T \mid \lambda x(t) \mid (t)t$
(Types)	T	::=	$B \mid \mathsf{Prop} \mid T \Longrightarrow S \mid X \mid \{x \in T.\varphi'\} \mid \{x.\varphi'\} \mid \Pi X.T \mid S \otimes T$
(atomic wff)	α	::=	$(t =_T s) \mid t \in K \mid t \cong_T s \mid {}^{\mathsf{T}}t$

$$\text{(wff)} \quad \varphi \quad ::= \quad \alpha \mid {\sim}\varphi \mid (\varphi \wedge \psi) \mid (\varphi \vee \psi) \mid (\varphi \rightarrow \psi) \mid (\varphi \leftrightarrow \psi) \mid (\forall x \varphi) \mid (\exists x \varphi) \mid (\forall X \varphi) \mid (\exists X \varphi)$$

where φ' is as defined in Section 5.5.2, and type variables X are intended to range only over non-polymorphic types.

5.6 Intensional Identity vs. Extensional Equivalence

There are two equality notions in PTCT. $t \cong_T s$ states that the terms t, s are extensionally equivalent in type T. Extensional equivalence is represented in the language of terms by $t \,\hat{\cong}_T\, s$. $t =_T s$ states that two terms are intensionally identical. The rules for intensional identity are essentially those of the $\lambda\alpha\beta\eta$-calculus. It is represented in the language of terms by $t \,\hat{=}_T\, s$. It is necessary to type the intensional identity predicate in order to avoid paradoxes when we introduce comprehension types.

The rules governing equivalence and identity are such that we are able to derive $t =_T s \rightarrow t \cong_T s$ for all types inhabited by t (s), but not $t \cong_T s \rightarrow t =_T s$. As a result, PTCT can sustain fine-grained intensional distinctions among provably equivalent propositions. Therefore, we avoid the reduction of logically equivalent expressions to the same intension, a reduction which holds in classical intensional semantics, without invoking impossible worlds. Moreover, we do so within a first-order system that uses a flexible Curry typing system rather than a higher-order logic with Church typing (as in FIL, Chapter 4).

We can construct PTCT analogues of the proofs that we gave in Chapter 4 of the validity of **IDENT** and the invalidity of **EXTEN**.

IDENT$_{\mathbf{PTCT}}$: $\forall x, y_{\in T}(x =_T y \rightarrow x \cong_T y)$
EXTEN$_{\mathbf{PTCT}}$: $\forall x, y_{\in T}(x \cong_T y \rightarrow x =_T y)$

The proof for **IDENT**$_{\mathbf{PTCT}}$ is as as follows:
$\sim \forall x, y((x, y \in T \wedge x =_T y) \rightarrow x \cong_T y)^*$
$\sim((a, b \in T \wedge a =_T b) \rightarrow a \cong_T b)^*$ (D-rule for $\forall$)

$a, b \in T \wedge a =_T b$*
$\sim(a \cong_T b)$ (*A* rule for Implication)
$a, b \in T$
$a =_T b$ (*A* rule for Conjunction)
$\sim(a \cong_T a)$ (*A* rule for Substitution)
$a \cong_T a$ (Equivalence (1)-reflexivity)
$\perp$ (contradiction)

The tree is closed. The following tableau provides a counterexample to **EXTEN**$_{\text{PTCT}}$:

$\sim \forall x, y((x, y \in T \wedge x \cong_T y) \rightarrow x =_T y)$*
$\sim((a, b \in T \wedge a \cong_T b) \rightarrow a =_T b)$* (*D*-rule for $\forall$)
$a, b \in T \wedge a \cong_T b$*
$\sim(a =_T b)$ (*A* rule for Implication)
$a, b \in T$
$a \cong_T b$ (*A* rule for Conjunction)

The tree is finished and open.

As in the case of FIL, the proof of the invalidity of **EXTEN**$_{\text{PTCT}}$ establishes the consistency of the proof theory for PTCT. However, it is important to note that, unlike FIL, this result demonstrates only the *weak consistency* of PTCT. Specifically, it shows that the tableau rules do not permit us to prove every sentence of PTCT, but it does not prove that there is no sentence of PTCT that generates a paradox. A proof that PTCT is free of paradox would demonstrate the *strong consistency* of the system. Strong consistency does not reduce to weak consistency in PTCT, as it does in FIL, because the former, in contrast to the latter, allows the internalization of the notion of proposition in an unstratified manner. So, for example, $t \in$ Prop for all $x \in$ Prop allows us to derive $(\hat{\forall} x \epsilon \text{Prop}) \in$ Prop. Here x in the first sentence ranges over all propositions, including the proposition in the second sentence, which we only know to be a proposition because Of the first sentence. This case of impredicativity does not generate a paradox because we have banned self-application (self-predication) in PTCT. In general, we have avoided paradox by placing constraints on functional application, type membership, and quantification over types. These conditions have permitted us to filter out paradoxes on a case-by-case basis. In order to arrive at a fully general proof of strong consistency, we need to show that paradox is not possible for any sentence within the system. Constructing such a proof is a complex affair, which we are still working on. We are confident that the proof will succeed, but we are forced to leave its completion and presentation to a future publication.

5.7 A Model Theory for PTCT

In order to give a model for PTCT, we first need a model of the untyped λ-calculus, which will provide the model for PTCT's language of terms. For convenience and simplicity we adopt Meyer's model (Meyer 1982) (readers should feel free to substitute their own favourite models of the untyped λ-calculus here).

5.7.1 Models of the (Extensional) λ-Calculus

Definition 6 (General Functional Models) *A functional model is a structure of the form* $\mathcal{D} = \langle D, [D \to D], \Phi, \Psi \rangle$ *where*
(1) D *is a non-empty set,*
(2) $[D \to D]$ *is some class of functions from D to D,*
(3) $\Phi : D \to [D \to D]$,
(4) $\Psi : [D \to D] \to D$,
(5) $\Psi(\Phi(d)) = d$ *for all* $d \in D$.

We can interpret the calculus using the following:

(129)
$$\begin{aligned} [\![x]\!]_g &= g(x) \\ [\![\lambda x t]\!]_g &= \Psi(\lambda d.[\![t]\!]_{g[d/x]}) \\ [\![ts]\!]_g &= \Phi([\![t]\!]_g)[\![s]\!]_g \end{aligned}$$

where g is an assignment function from variables to elements of D. This interpretation exploits the fact that Φ maps every element of D into a corresponding function from D to D, and Ψ maps functions from D to D into elements of D.

Note that we require functions of the form $\lambda d.[\![t]\!]_{g[d/x]}$ to be in the class $[D \to D]$ to ensure that the interpretation is well defined. Here we are just following Meyer (1982).

In the case where we permit constant terms, then we add the clause

(130) $[\![c]\!]_g = i(c)$

where i assigns elements of D to constants.

Theorem 8 *If $t = s$ in the extensional untyped λ-calculus (with η), then $[\![t]\!]_g = [\![s]\!]_g$ for each assignment g.*

Proof: By induction on the derivations. □

A model $\mathcal{M}$ of PTCT is constructed on the basis of a simple extensional model of the untyped λ-calculus (Barendregt 1984; Meyer 1982; Turner 1997), with additional structure added to capture the type rules and the relation between the sublanguages of PTCT.

Definition 7 (Model of PTCT) *A model of PTCT is $\mathcal{M} = \langle \mathcal{D}, \mathsf{T}, \mathsf{P}, \mathsf{B}, \mathcal{B}, \mathcal{T}', \mathcal{T} \rangle$, where*
(1) $\mathcal{D}$ is a model of the λ-calculus
(2) $\mathsf{T} : D \to \{0, 1\}$ models the truth predicate ^{T}
(3) $\mathsf{P} \subset D$ models the class of propositions
(4) $\mathsf{B} \subset D$ models the class of basic individuals
(5) $\mathcal{B}(\mathsf{B})$ is a set of sets whose elements partition B into equivalence classes of individuals
(6) $\mathcal{T}' \subset \mathcal{T}$ models the class of non-polymorphic types
(7) $\mathcal{T} \subset D$ models the class of types
with sufficient structural constraints on T, P, $\mathcal{T}$ and $\mathcal{T}'$ to validate the tableau rules of PTCT.

In the following, we give the structural constraints required to sustain the proof theory given in Section 5.3.

5.7.2 Types

Types can be interpreted as subsets of D. To ensure that polymorphic types are predicative (i.e. to avoid an implicit circularity in their definition), quantification is only allowed over non-polymorphic types.

To give a first-order account of type quantification, we consider the interpretation of term *representations* of types. We take types in PTCT to denote terms in $\mathcal{T} \subset D$. If type T in PTCT denotes an individual $S \in \mathcal{T}$, the underlying type (or set of individuals) will be denoted by $\mathcal{E}S$.

The types in the model, and the interpretation of PTCT's types are specified by the following rules:

(131) (a) For all $t \in \mathcal{T}, \mathcal{E}t \subset D$
(b) $[\![B]\!]_{g,\tau} \in \mathcal{T}'$
(c) $[\![\mathsf{Prop}]\!]_{g,\tau} \in \mathcal{T}'$
(d) $[\![X]\!]_{g,\tau} = \tau(X) \in \mathcal{T}'$
(e) If $[\![S]\!]_{g,\tau}, [\![U]\!]_{g,\tau} \in \mathcal{T}'$, then $[\![S \Longrightarrow U]\!]_{g,\tau} \in \mathcal{T}'$
(f) If $[\![S]\!]_{g,\tau} \in \mathcal{T}'$ and $[\![\ulcorner\varphi'\urcorner]\!]_{g,\tau} \in \mathsf{P}$, then $[\![\{x \in S.\varphi'\]\!]_{g,\tau} \in \mathcal{T}'$
(g) If $[\![\ulcorner\varphi'\urcorner]\!]_{g,\tau} \in \mathsf{Prop}$, then $[\![\{x\varphi'\}]\!]_{g,\tau} \in \mathcal{T}'$
(h) If $[\![S]\!]_{g,\tau} \in \mathcal{T}'$, then $[\![\Pi X.S]\!]_{g,\tau} \in \mathcal{T}$
(i) If $[\![S]\!]_{g,\tau}, [\![T]\!]_{g,\tau} \in \mathcal{T}'$, then $[\![S \otimes T]\!]_{g,\tau} \in \mathcal{T}'$
(j) $\mathcal{E}[\![B]\!]_{g,\tau} = \mathsf{B} \subseteq D$
(k) $\mathcal{E}[\![\mathsf{Prop}]\!]_{g,\tau} = \mathsf{P} \subseteq D$
(l) $\mathcal{E}[\![S \Longrightarrow U]\!]_{g,\tau} = \{d \in D : \forall e \in \mathcal{E}[\![S]\!]_{g,\tau}.(\Phi(d))e \in \mathcal{E}[\![U]\!]_{g,\tau}\}$
(m) $\mathcal{E}[\![\{x \in S.\varphi'\}]\!]_{g,\tau} = \{d \in \mathcal{E}[\![S]\!]_{g,\tau}.\mathcal{M}_{g[d/x],\tau} \models \varphi'\}$
(n) $\mathcal{E}[\![\{x.\varphi'\}]\!]_{g,\tau} = \{d \in D.\mathcal{M}_{g[d/x],\tau} \models \varphi'\}$
(o) $\mathcal{E}[\![\Pi X.S]\!]_{g,\tau} = \{d \in D : \forall U \in \mathcal{T}'.d \in \mathcal{E}[\![S]\!]_{g,\tau[U/X]}\}$
(p) $\mathcal{E}[\![S \otimes T]\!]_{g,\tau} = \{d \in D : \{d' \in D : d \in \mathcal{E}[\![S]\!]_{g,\tau}$ and $d' \in \mathcal{E}[\![T]\!]_{g,\tau}\}\}$

Here, τ is an assignment from type variables to elements of $\mathcal{T}$, $\ulcorner\cdot\urcorner$ is as defined in Section 5.5.2, and Φ is as defined in the Meyer model of the untyped λ-calculus (Section 5.7.1).

5.7.3 Propositions

The typing rules for Prop are supported by the following structural constraints on models:

(132) (a) If $[\![t]\!]_{g,\tau} \in \mathsf{P}$, then $[\![\hat{\sim} t]\!]_{g,\tau} \in \mathsf{P}$.
(b) If $[\![t]\!]_{g,\tau} \in \mathsf{P}$ and $[\![s]\!]_{g,\tau} \in \mathsf{P}$, then $[\![t \mathbin{\hat{\wedge}} s]\!]_{g,\tau} \in \mathsf{P}$.

(c) if $[\![t]\!]_{g,\tau} \in \mathsf{P}$ and $[\![s]\!]_{g,\tau} \in \mathsf{P}$, then $[\![t \mathbin{\hat{\vee}} s]\!]_{g,\tau} \in \mathsf{P}$.
(d) if $[\![t]\!]_{g,\tau} \in \mathsf{P}$, and $[\![s]\!]_{g,\tau} \in \mathsf{P}$, then $[\![t \mathbin{\hat{\rightarrow}} s]\!]_{g,\tau} \in \mathsf{P}$.
(e) if $[\![t]\!]_{g,\tau} \in \mathsf{P}$ and $[\![s]\!]_{g,\tau} \in \mathsf{P}$ then $[\![t \mathbin{\hat{\leftrightarrow}} s]\!]_{g,\tau} \in \mathsf{P}$.
(f) If $[\![S]\!]_{g,\tau} \in \mathcal{T}$, and $[\![t]\!]_{g[d/x],\tau} \in \mathsf{P}$ for all $d \in \mathcal{E}[\![S]\!]_{g,\tau}$, then $[\![\hat{\forall} x \epsilon S(t)]\!]_{g,\tau} \in \mathsf{P}$.
(g) If $[\![S]\!]_{g,\tau} \in \mathcal{T}$, and $[\![t]\!]_{g[d/x],\tau} \in \mathsf{P}$ for all $d \in \mathcal{E}[\![S]\!]_{g,\tau}$, then $[\![\hat{\exists} x \epsilon S(t)]\!]_{g,\tau} \in \mathsf{P}$.
(h) If $[\![S]\!]_{g,\tau} \in \mathcal{T}$, then $[\![t \mathrel{\hat{\cong}_S} s]\!]_{g,\tau} \in \mathsf{P}$ iff $[\![s]\!]_{g,\tau}, [\![t]\!]_{g,\tau} \in \mathcal{E}[\![S]\!]_{g,\tau}$.
(i) If $[\![S]\!]_{g,\tau} \in \mathcal{T}$, then $[\![t \mathrel{\hat{=}_S} s]\!]_{g,\tau} \in \mathsf{P}$ iff $[\![s]\!]_{g,\tau}, [\![t]\!]_{g,\tau} \in \mathcal{E}[\![S]\!]_{g,\tau}$.

5.7.4 Truth

The rules for ^{T} are supported by the following conditions:

(133) (a) If $[\![t]\!]_{g,\tau} \in \mathsf{P}$, then $\mathsf{T}([\![\hat{\sim} t]\!]_{g,\tau}) = 1$ iff $\mathsf{T}([\![t]\!]_{g,\tau}) = 0$.
(b) If $[\![t]\!]_{g,\tau} \in \mathsf{P}$ and $[\![s]\!]_{g,\tau} \in \mathsf{P}$, then $\mathsf{T}([\![t \mathbin{\hat{\wedge}} s]\!]_{g,\tau}) = 1$ iff $\mathsf{T}([\![t]\!]_{g,\tau}) = 1$ and $\mathsf{T}([\![s]\!]_{g,\tau}) = 1$.
(c) If $[\![t]\!]_{g,\tau} \in \mathsf{P}$ and $[\![s]\!]_{g,\tau} \in \mathsf{P}$, then $\mathsf{T}([\![t \mathbin{\hat{\vee}} s]\!]_{g,\tau}) = 1$ iff either $\mathsf{T}([\![t]\!]_{g,\tau}) = 1$ or $\mathsf{T}([\![s]\!]_{g,\tau}) = 1$.
(d) If $[\![t]\!]_{g,\tau} \in \mathsf{P}$ and $[\![s]\!]_{g,\tau} \in \mathsf{P}$, then $\mathsf{T}([\![t \mathbin{\hat{\rightarrow}} s]\!]_{g,\tau}) = 1$ iff either $\mathsf{T}([\![t]\!]_{g,\tau}) = 0$ or $\mathsf{T}([\![s]\!]_{g,\tau}) = 1$.
(e) If $[\![t]\!]_{g,\tau} \in \mathsf{P}$ and $[\![s]\!]_{g,\tau} \in \mathsf{P}$, then $\mathsf{T}([\![t \mathbin{\hat{\leftrightarrow}} s]\!]_{g,\tau}) = 1$ iff $[\![t]\!]_{g,\tau} = [\![s]\!]_{g,\tau}$.
(f) If $[\![S]\!]_{g,\tau} \in \mathcal{T}$ and $[\![t]\!]_{g[d/x],\tau} \in \mathsf{P}$ for all $d \in \mathcal{E}[\![S]\!]_{g,\tau}$, then $\mathsf{T}([\![\hat{\forall} x \epsilon S(t)]\!]_{g,\tau}) = 1$ iff $\mathsf{T}([\![t]\!]_{g[d/x],\tau}) = 1$ for all $d \in \mathcal{E}[\![S]\!]_{g,\tau}$.
(g) if $[\![S]\!]_{g,\tau} \in \mathcal{T}$ and $[\![t]\!]_{g[d/x],\tau} \in \mathsf{P}$ for all $d \in \mathcal{E}[\![S]\!]_{g,\tau}$, then $\mathsf{T}([\![\hat{\exists} x \epsilon S(t)]\!]_{g,\tau}) = 1$ iff $\mathsf{T}([\![t]\!]_{g[d/x],\tau}) = 1$ for some $d \in [\![S]\!]_{g,\tau}$.
(h) i. If $[\![t]\!]_{g,\tau}, [\![s]\!]_{g,\tau} \in \mathsf{B}$, then $\mathsf{T}([\![t \mathrel{\hat{\cong}_{\mathsf{B}}} s]\!]_{g,\tau}) = 1$ iff there is a set S such that $S \in \mathcal{B}(\mathsf{B})$ and $[\![t]\!]_{g,\tau}, [\![s]\!]_{g,\tau} \in S$.[31]

[31] This condition permits individual constants in PTCT to be extensionally equivalent but intensionally distinct. It covers cases of coextensional names like *Tully* and *Cicero*, which are naturally construed as different in intension.

ii. If $[\![t]\!]_{g,\tau}, [\![s]\!]_{g,\tau} \in \mathsf{P}$, then $\mathsf{T}([\![t \hat{\cong}_{\mathsf{Prop}} s]\!]_{g,\tau}) = 1$ iff $\mathsf{T}([\![t]\!]_{g,\tau}) = \mathsf{T}([\![s]\!]_{g,\tau})$.

iii. If $[\![t]\!]_{g,\tau}, [\![s]\!]_{g,\tau} \in [\![S \Longrightarrow U]\!]_{g,\tau}$,
where $[\![S]\!]_{g,\tau}, [\![U]\!]_{g,\tau} \in \mathcal{T}$,
then $\mathsf{T}([\![t \hat{\cong}_{(S \Longrightarrow U)} s]\!]_{g,\tau}) = 1$
iff $\mathsf{T}([\![tx \hat{\cong}_U sx]\!]_{g[d/x],\tau}) = 1$ for all $d \in \mathcal{E}[\![S]\!]_{g,\tau}$.

(i) If $[\![t]\!]_{g,\tau}, [\![s]\!]_{g,\tau} \in \mathcal{E}[\![S]\!]_{g,\tau}$, then $\mathsf{T}([\![t \hat{=}_S s]\!]_{g,\tau}) = 1$ iff $[\![t]\!]_{g,\tau} = [\![s]\!]_{g,\tau}$.

(j) If $\mathsf{T}([\![t]\!]_{g,\tau}) = 1$ then $[\![t]\!]_{g,\tau} \in \mathsf{P}$.

Note that we give no rules for the extensional equivalence of comprehension types, separation types or polymorphic types. Such equivalences can be problematic.

5.7.5 Well-Formed Formulae

The language of wffs can now be given truth conditions.

(134)

(134)	$\mathcal{M}_{g,\tau} \models s =_T t$	iff $[\![t]\!]_{g,\tau}, [\![s]\!]_{g,\tau} \in \mathcal{E}[\![T]\!]_{g,\tau}$ and $[\![t]\!]_{g,\tau} = [\![s]\!]_{g,\tau}$
	$\mathcal{M}_{g,\tau} \models s \cong_T t$	iff $\mathsf{T}([\![s]\!]_{g,\tau} \hat{\cong}_T [\![t]\!]_{g,\tau}) = 1$
	$\mathcal{M}_{g,\tau} \models s \cong_{\mathsf{Prop}} t$	iff $[\![s]\!]_{g,\tau}, [\![t]\!]_{g,\tau} \in \mathsf{P}$ and $\mathcal{M}_{g,\tau} \models {}^{\mathsf{T}}s \leftrightarrow {}^{\mathsf{T}}t$
	$\mathcal{M}_{g,\tau} \models s \cong_{(T \Longrightarrow \mathsf{Prop})} t$	iff $[\![s]\!]_{g,\tau}, [\![t]\!]_{g,\tau} \in [\![T \Longrightarrow \mathsf{Prop}]\!]_{g,\tau}$ and for all $x \in T$, $\mathcal{M}_{g,\tau} \models {}^{\mathsf{T}}sx \leftrightarrow {}^{\mathsf{T}}tx$ (x not free in s, t)
	$\mathcal{M}_{g,\tau} \models {}^{\mathsf{T}}(t)$	iff $\mathsf{T}([\![t]\!]_{g,\tau}) = 1$
	$\mathcal{M}_{g,\tau} \models t \in T$	iff $[\![t]\!]_{g,\tau} \in \mathcal{E}[\![T]\!]_{g,\tau}$[32]
	$\mathcal{M}_{g,\tau} \models \sim\varphi$	iff $\mathcal{M}_{g,\tau} \not\models \varphi$
	$\mathcal{M}_{g,\tau} \models \varphi \wedge \psi$	iff $\mathcal{M}_{g,\tau} \models \varphi$ and $\mathcal{M}_{g,\tau} \models \psi$
	$\mathcal{M}_{g,\tau} \models \varphi \vee \psi$	iff $\mathcal{M}_{g,\tau} \models \varphi$ or $\mathcal{M}_{g,\tau} \models \psi$
	$\mathcal{M}_{g,\tau} \models \varphi \rightarrow \psi$	iff $\mathcal{M}_{g,\tau} \not\models \varphi$ or $\mathcal{M}_{g,\tau} \models \psi$
	$\mathcal{M}_{g,\tau} \models \varphi \leftrightarrow \psi$	iff $\mathcal{M}_{g,\tau} \models \varphi$ exactly when $\mathcal{M}_{g,\tau} \models \psi$
	$\mathcal{M}_{g,\tau} \models \forall x\varphi$	iff for all $d \in D$, $\mathcal{M}_{g[d/x],\tau} \models \varphi$
	$\mathcal{M}_{g,\tau} \models \exists x\varphi$	iff for some $d \in D$, $\mathcal{M}_{g[d/x],\tau} \models \varphi$
	$\mathcal{M}_{g,\tau} \models \forall X\varphi$	iff for all $S \in \mathcal{T}'$, $\mathcal{M}_{g,\tau[S/X]} \models \varphi$
	$\mathcal{M}_{g,\tau} \models \exists X\varphi$	iff for some $S \in \mathcal{T}'$, $\mathcal{M}_{g,\tau[S/X]} \models \varphi$

32 Syntactic constraints on T guarantee that $[\![T]\!]_{g,\tau} \in \mathcal{T}$.

Here, type quantification is restricted to non-polymorphic types. Type variables are already constrained to denote types in $\mathcal{T}'$.

Definition 8 (Validity) *A wff φ of PTCT is* valid *iff $\mathcal{M}_{g,\tau} \models \varphi$ for all models $\mathcal{M}$ and all assignment functions g, τ.*

Theorem 9 (Soundness of PTCT) *If PTCT φ, then φ is valid.*

Proof: To prove that the tableau proof procedure for PTCT is sound, we have to prove the following lemma:

Lemma 1 *If the initial sentence S of a tableau T is satisfied in a model $\mathcal{M}$ for PTCT, then there is an open (possibly infinite) path P in T in which every full sentence in P is satisfied.*

Lemma 1 follows by induction on the downward correctness of the tableau rules relative to the model theory of PTCT. For each full sentence F in P, if F is true in $\mathcal{M}$, then the rules of the model theory ensure that the sentences in the extension of the open path derived from F by application of the tableau rules are also satisfied in $\mathcal{M}$. We illustrate downward correctness of the tableau rules with three examples, one for each type of rule.

Rules for Wffs: Universal Quantification

The truth condition given in (134) for universal quantification over individuals entails that if $\forall x\varphi$ is true in $\mathcal{M}$, then $\varphi^{x/c}$ is true in $\mathcal{M}$ for every individual constant c such that $i(c) \in \mathcal{D}$.

Type Inference Rules: General Function Spaces

(131l) and the truth condition for type membership formulas given in (134) entail that if $t \in (S \Longrightarrow T)$ and $t' \in S$ are true in $\mathcal{M}$, then $tt' \in T$ is true in $\mathcal{M}$.

Truth Rules: Conjunction

The truth conditions for $^{\mathsf{T}}(t)$ and $\varphi \wedge \psi$ in (134), and (133b) entail that if $^{\mathsf{T}}(s \mathbin{\hat{\wedge}} t)$ and $s, t \in \mathsf{Prop}$ are true in $\mathcal{M}$, then $^{\mathsf{T}}s \wedge {}^{\mathsf{T}}t$ is true in $\mathcal{M}$.

From Lemma 1 it follows that if the tableau for a formula S is closed, then S is not satisfiable in a model of PTCT. Therefore, if there is a proof of S (i.e. the tableau for $\sim S$ is closed), then S is satisfied in all models of PTCT. □

Theorem 10 (Completeness of PTCT) *If φ is valid, then PTCT φ.*

Proof: To prove that the tableau proof procedure for PTCT is complete we must prove the following lemma:

Lemma 2 *If there is an open (possibly infinite) path in a tableau for a sentence S, then S is satisfiable in a model of PTCT.*

Lemma 2 follows by induction on the upward correctness of the tableau rules relative to the model theory for PTCT. For each set Γ of formulas in an extension of an open path derived by the application of the tableau rules to a formula F, if the elements of Γ are true in a model $\mathcal{M}$, then the definition of the model theory ensures that F is satisfiable in $\mathcal{M}$. We illustrate the upward correctness of the tableau rules with the same examples that we used for downward correctness. In these illustrations correctness runs in the opposite direction, from the hypothesis that the conclusions of the rule are true in $\mathcal{M}$ to the result that its premise(s) are satisfiable in $\mathcal{M}$.

Rules for Wffs: Universal Quantification

The truth condition given in (134) for universal quantification over individuals entails that if $\varphi^{x/c}$ is true in $\mathcal{M}$ for every individual constant c that appears in the open path, where $i(c) \in \mathcal{D}$, then $\forall x\varphi$ is satisfiable in $\mathcal{M}$.

Type Inference Rules: General Function Spaces

(131(l)) and the truth condition for type membership formulas given in (134) entail that if $tt' \in T$ is true in $\mathcal{M}$, then $t \in (S \Longrightarrow T)$ and $t' \in S$ are true in $\mathcal{M}$.

Truth Rules: Conjunction

The truth conditions for $^{\mathsf{T}}(t)$ and $\varphi \wedge \psi$ in (134), together with (133(b)) and (133(j)) entail that if $^{\mathsf{T}}s \wedge {}^{\mathsf{T}}t$ is true in $\mathcal{M}$, then $^{\mathsf{T}}(s \mathbin{\hat{\wedge}} t)$ and $s, t \in$ Prop are true in $\mathcal{M}$.

Lemma 2 entails that if a branch B in a tableau for S is open, then all the sentences in B, including S, are satisfiable in a model of

PTCT. It follows that if S is valid ($\sim S$ is not satisfiable in a model of PTCT), then there is a tableau proof of S. □

5.8 Types and Properties

On initial examination, it appears that there are parallels between properties and types in PTCT, along the following lines:

(135) (a) $x\epsilon T \approx T(x)$
(b) $(T \Longrightarrow S) \approx \hat{\forall} x\epsilon T(S(x)) \approx \hat{\forall} x(T(x) \hat{\rightarrow} S(x))$
(c) $\{x \in T.\varphi'\} \approx \lambda x(x\epsilon T \mathbin{\hat{\wedge}} \ulcorner\varphi'\urcorner) \approx \lambda x(T(x) \mathbin{\hat{\wedge}} \ulcorner\varphi'\urcorner)$
(d) $\{x.\varphi'\} \approx \lambda x(\ulcorner\varphi'\urcorner)$

There is a sense in which types could be thought of as properties of type $\Delta \Longrightarrow$ Prop, although as we have seen above (Section 5.5), adding the universal type directly to PTCT is problematic.

This apparent similarity between types and properties leads to the notion of the *property-theoretic definability* of a type.

Definition 9 (Property-Theoretic Definability of a Type) *A type T is definable as an unrestricted property p iff $\forall x(x \in T \leftrightarrow {}^{\mathsf{T}}p(x))$, where an unrestricted property is one that forms a proposition with any argument.*

If we allow type membership to be represented by predication in this way, then we have effectively allowed free-floating type judgements in the language of terms, of the form $x\epsilon T$. We might consider axiomatizing the behaviour of free-floating type judgements directly as follows:

(136) $\mathsf{Type}(T) \rightarrow (x\epsilon T) \in \mathsf{Prop}$
(137) $\mathsf{Type}(T) \rightarrow {}^{\mathsf{T}}(x\epsilon T) \leftrightarrow x \in T$

We could add further constraints to these axioms, such as requiring that the term on the left of the membership symbol is not a type.

Unfortunately, allowing both free-floating type judgements, and full property-theoretic definability of types leads to a paradox in the case of the type Prop.[33]

Theorem 11 Prop *cannot appear in free-floating type judgements of the form* $x\epsilon$Prop.

Proof: Consider the term

$$R = \lambda x(\hat{\sim}(xx\epsilon\mathsf{Prop}))$$

Assuming that Type(Prop), then we can show that $\forall x(R(x) \in$ Prop). Therefore $RR \in$ Prop. The axioms governing truth then allow us to show that $^{\mathsf{T}}(RR) \leftrightarrow (RR \notin$ Prop), which yields a contradiction. □

Corollary 2 Prop *has no property-theoretic definition.*

These problems with free-floating type judgements also indicate why we require intensional identity to be typed. If it were not, then we could define free-floating type judgements as follows.

(138) $x\epsilon T =_{\mathsf{def}} \hat{\exists} y\epsilon T(x \hat{=} y)$

As it stands, we require the type of y to be imposed independently of the identity statement.

5.9 Separation Types and Internal Type Judgements

The preceding discussion suggests that it is not possible to represent free-floating type judgements in PTCT's language of terms. This is problematic, as it would be convenient to be able to use such judgements in the analysis of certain natural language phenomena, such as ellipsis (Chapter 7). However, as we shall now see, there are some kinds of type judgements that *can* be incorporated into the language of terms. Further more, it turns out

33 Such paradoxes would also arise if we were to treat truth as a type.

that these judgements, and the context in which they can felicitously appear, correspond to the way we wish to use them in the type-theoretic analysis of ellipsis.

The types in question are separation types. Recall that these types have the following form:

(139) $\{x \in T.\varphi'\}$

where φ' is an internally representable wff as defined in Section 5.5.2.

As previously described, a term z is a member of this type under the following circumstances.

(140) $z \in \{x \in T.\varphi'\} \leftrightarrow (z \in T \wedge \varphi'[z/x])$

φ' is term representable (it contains no free-floating type judgements), and so the only part of the right-side of this equivalence that is not term representable is $z \in T$. If we knew independently that $z \in T$, then we would have the following:

(141) $z \in \{x \in T.\ulcorner\varphi'\urcorner\} \leftrightarrow \varphi'[z/x]$

This statement is equivalent to

(142) $z \in T \rightarrow (z \in \{x \in T.\varphi'\} \leftrightarrow \varphi'[z/x])$

Observe that $\varphi'[z/x]$ is equivalent to ${}^{\mathsf{T}}((\lambda x\ulcorner\varphi'\urcorner)z)$. Thus, it turns out that $z \in \{x \in T.\varphi'\}$ is equivalent to ${}^{\mathsf{T}}((\lambda x\ulcorner\varphi'\urcorner)z)$, in the event that $z \in T$.

We conclude that it is safe to have a *restricted* form of free-floating type judgement in the language of terms. We use the symbol $\hat{\in}$ to represent a restricted type membership relation of this kind. We can axiomatize it in the usual way, describing when such type judgements are propositions, and when they are true propositions.

(143) $t \in S \rightarrow (t \mathrel{\hat{\in}} \{x \in S.\varphi'\}) \in \mathsf{Prop}$

and

(144) $t \in S \rightarrow ({}^{\mathsf{T}}(t \mathrel{\hat{\in}} \{x \in S.\varphi'\}) \leftrightarrow \varphi'[t/x])$

Conceptually, this internalizable type judgement can be thought of as exploiting a combination of the notion of a *universe* or *small type* as used in MLTT (Martin-Löf 1982, 1984) and Frege Structures (Aczel 1980) (where only some types can appear in internal type judgements) with Turner's S5-like treatment of the internalization of troublesome predicates, such as those for propositions and truth in PT (Section 3.4.5). The internal type judgement only 'makes sense' if we already know something about the type of the term t. There is a clear connection between this approach to accommodating restricted free-floating type judgements and our use of typed identity and equivalence predicates to avoid paradox. They are both instances of the same strategy.

So internal type judgements $t \mathrel{\hat{\in}} S$ are felicitous, provided S is a separation type $\{x \in T.\varphi'\}$, and that we are in a context where it can be shown independently that $t \in T$. Fortuitously, these are precisely the constraints that are met by the type-theoretic analysis of ellipsis in Chapter 7.

There is a choice about how to incorporate these observations into PTCT. We could change the language, add new rules and revise the model, or we can take expressions involving $t \mathrel{\hat{\in}} \{x \in T.\varphi\}$ – where we know $t \in T$ – to be 'syntactic sugar' for an equivalent representation that does not involve these new judgements, namely $(\lambda x(\ulcorner\varphi'\urcorner))t$.

On the former approach, one way of proceeding is to add the logical constant $\hat{\in}$ to the language of terms, and to adopt the the following tableau rule to determine that a judgement is felicitous.[34]

Internal Separation Types

$$\begin{array}{c} \ulcorner\varphi'\urcorner \in \mathsf{Prop} \\ | \\ z \mathrel{\hat{\in}} \{x \in T.\varphi'\} \in \mathsf{Prop} \end{array} \qquad \textit{where } z \in T$$

34 An alternative would be to 'overload' the existing ϵ constant.

The following two rules determine when the judgement is true:

Internal Separation Types

$$\begin{array}{c} {}^{\mathsf{T}}(z \mathrel{\hat{\in}} \{x \in T.\varphi'\})^* \quad \textit{where } z \in T \\ | \\ \ulcorner\varphi'\urcorner[z/x] \end{array}$$

Negated Internal Separation Types

$$\begin{array}{c} \sim {}^{\mathsf{T}}(z \mathrel{\hat{\in}} \{x \in T.\varphi'\})^* \quad \textit{where } z \in T \\ | \\ \sim \ulcorner\varphi'\urcorner[z/x] \end{array}$$

On the alternative approach, we can use the following definition:

Definition 10 (Restricted Free-Floating Type Judgements) *In the context where $t \in T$, terms of the form $t \mathrel{\hat{\in}} \{x \in T.\varphi\}$ are taken to be 'syntactic sugar' for $(\lambda x(\ulcorner\varphi'\urcorner))t$.*

For presentational reasons, we here adopt the latter approach. In places we also use the notation $\in$ for $\hat{\in}$ where the context makes it clear what is meant.

Whichever approach is taken, it is possible to revise our recursive definition of translation for term representable wffs to terms so that it includes a translation rule for unproblematic type judgements, for example[35]

(145) $\ulcorner a \in \{x \in T.\varphi'\}\urcorner = a \mathrel{\hat{\in}} \{x \in T.\varphi'\}$

In the case of logics that adopt the Church-typed λ-calculus, such as FIL (Chapter 4), the connection between separation types and predicates is more direct. We can simply define the separation type as a typed λ-abstract.

(146) $\{x \in T.\varphi'\} =_{\mathsf{def}} \lambda x_{\in T}.\varphi'$

Of course, we then lose the flexibility of the Curry-typed system.

35 The original recursive translation is defined only for term-representable wffs. Adding this new rule for type judgements gives a translation whose result is specified for some non-representable wffs, namely, type judgements of the form $a \in \{x \in T.\varphi'\}$ where it cannot be shown that $a \in T$, but the result will not be a proposition. If the translation procedure is to be constrained to avoid such cases, then it needs to be revised so that it keeps track of the relevant typing context.

5.10 Truth as a Type

We could contemplate treating truth as a type, rather than a predicate in the language of wffs. In this case, a new type T would be added to the language of types, and the wff $^{\mathsf{T}}t$ become redundant. Its occurrence could be replaced by $t \in \mathsf{T}$.

In general, such a move is fraught with potential problems. The interested reader who is keen to pursue this option must ensure that this move does not allow the derivation of paradoxes that render the logic inconsistent.

5.11 Conclusion

We have constructed a first-order fine-grained intensional logic with flexible Curry typing, PTCT, for the semantic representation of natural languages. PTCT contains typed predicates for intensional identity and extensional equality. Its proof theory permits us to prove that identity of intension entails identity of extension, but that the converse does not hold.

The theory can be distinguished from Aczel's Frege Structures (Aczel 1980) and related, weakly typed theories of properties (PT) (Turner 1988) in two ways. First, there is an explicit notion of polymorphic type within the theory, which is more appropriate for natural language semantics than the universal type of PT. Second, the type Prop can appear in intensional representations of propositions. This allows us to express the fact that, for example, the universal quantification in the term representation of statements of the form *John believes everything that Mary believes* ranges only over propositions (see Section 9.4). In PT, this requirement can only be expressed as an external constraint (Turner 1997).

We have provided a model theory for PTCT using extensional models for the untyped λ-calculus enriched with interpretations of Curry types. The restrictions that we impose on separation types, comprehension types, quantification over types, and the relation between the three sublanguages of PTCT ensure that it remains a first-order system in which its enriched expressive power comes largely through quantification over terms and the representation of types as terms within the language.

Unlike alternative hyperintensionalist frameworks that have been proposed, this logic distinguishes among provably equivalent propositions without resorting to impossible worlds to sustain the distinction. The incorporation of Curry typing into the logic allows us to sustain weak polymorphism. We will see in the next chapter that subtypes also permit us to develop a uniform, dynamic type-theoretic account of pronominal anaphora and ellipsis resolution, with wide empirical coverage. This application will illustrate the expressive power of the system to express complex semantic phenomena of natural language in a straightforward and formally integrated way.

Chapter 6

Number Theory and Cardinality

The two theories that we have presented so far, FIL (Chapter 4) and PTCT (Chapter 5), can be used to represent simple natural language statements. The statements can only refer to singular individuals, and can only use classical notions of quantification. This is inadequate on various grounds. There is no account of plurals and mass terms, for example, or anaphora and ellipsis.

Some of these phenomena, such as anaphora and ellipsis, can be addressed by considering the translation process from natural language into the formal representation (Chapter 7). Others, such as plurals and mass terms, require extensions to the theories.

This chapter is concerned with the latter case, where an extension to both theories is required. There are many extensions required to cover a wider range of natural language statements. We limit ourselves to the example of numbers and cardinality. The reason for this choice is not just that it has wide applicability, but also because it is an example that forces us to reflect on the balance between expressive power and formal strength.

First, we introduce a problem that illustrates that we need a notion of number and cardinality in a theory of natural language semantics, even for natural language statements that are not explicitly about numbers. Next, we reprise Peano arithmetic, then we extend both FIL and PTCT to include Peano arithmetic. This is used to provide an analysis of the proportional cardinality quantifier *most* within both theories.

Finally, we introduce Presburger arithmetic, which although weaker than Peano arithmetic, seems sufficiently expressive to cope with the phenomena of interest without resulting in a theory that is incomplete.

6.1 Proportional Cardinality Quantifiers

Quantifiers such as *most* must be treated as non-logical constants, in the sense that they cannot be represented in terms of the usual universal and existential quantifiers. If we say

Most children sing.

this is true when the number of children who sing is greater than the number of children who do not sing. Equivalently (at least in a classical system), it is true when the number of children who sing is at least half the total number of children.

This requires us to make judgements about the cardinality of the sets *children* and *children who sing*. In an intensional theory, this corresponds to judgements about the cardinality of the extension of the representations of these notions, or of the sets/types that are characterized by them.

To express such judgements, we need to add a number theory to the semantic formalism, and then add a notion of cardinality. To this end, we present Peano arithmetic, and show how it can be incorporated within both FIL and PTCT. Then we use this number theory to define cardinality.

It is possible to express the truth conditions of logical quantifiers in terms of cardinality. For example, the truth conditions of

Some children sing.

can be expressed as the requirement that the cardinality of the collection of singing children is at least one. The truth conditions of

Every child sang.

can be stated as the cardinality of the children who sang is equal to the cardinality of the collection of children.

When it comes to implementation, this is perhaps not the most efficient way of dealing with logical quantification, however, these ideas can be exploited to clarify the exposition of our treatment of anaphora and ellipsis (Chapter 7).

To some extent, it is a matter of taste whether to formulate cardinality directly in terms of properties (p) or in terms of sets, or types, characterized by those properties ($\{x : \lambda x(p)\}$ or $\{x\epsilon B.\lambda x(p)\}$). In the following, we choose to give a property-theoretic formulation of cardinality in FIL, and both a property-theoretic and type-theoretic formulation for PTCT. The latter is assumed in Chapter 7.

The question arises as to the formal power of such theories. Adding Peano arithmetic to a theory increases its power. It also renders the theory incomplete.

One interesting observation is that the representation of the 'sets' required for proportionality quantifiers, and quantification over them, does not by itself necessarily require a higher-order logic, if the sets of interest are all characterized by properties that can be represented by first-order terms, for example.

As we shall see in Section 6.7, it is possible to consider adopting a weaker, decidable, number theory (such as Presburger arithmetic (Presburger 1929)). Such theories may be adequate for many cases of proportional cardinality quantifiers. If we are interested in limiting the formal power of PTCT, for example, such moves would help ensure that we have a recursively enumerable theory that can cope with proportional cardinality quantifiers.[36]

[36] Yoad Winter has suggested to us that, alternatively, we may be able to sustain completeness of PTCT with an intensional number theory in which the Peano axioms are modified to generate only bounded sets of natural numbers. He points out that a weak number theory of this kind may be sufficient for natural language semantics.

6.2 Peano Arithmetic

The usual axioms for Peano arithmetic are the following:

(147) (a) $\sim \exists x(succ(x) = 0)$
(b) $succ(x) = succ(y) \rightarrow x = y$
(c) $x = y \rightarrow succ(x) = succ(y)$
(d) $zero(0) = \mathrm{t}$
(e) $zero(succ(x)) = \mathrm{f}$
(f) $zero(\perp) = \perp$
(g) $pred(succ(x)) = x$
(h) $pred(0) = \perp$
(i) $pred(\perp) = \perp$

In order to be able to reason about expressions involving numbers, the following axiom schema for induction can be adopted:

(148) $(\varphi[0] \wedge \forall x(\varphi[x] \rightarrow \varphi[succ(x)])) \rightarrow \forall x(\varphi[x])$

It is possible to find terms in the untyped λ-calculus that, when assigned the roles of *zero*, *succ*, *pred* and 0, satisfy the Peano axioms. A collection of such terms that satisfy these axioms can be viewed as an implementation of Peano arithmetic. Here is a concrete example:

(149) (a) $0 =_{\mathrm{def}} \lambda x.x$
(b) $succ =_{\mathrm{def}} \lambda x \langle \mathrm{f}, x \rangle$
(c) $zero =_{\mathrm{def}} \lambda u(u\mathrm{t})$
(d) $pred =_{\mathrm{def}} \lambda x(zero(x) \longrightarrow \perp, x(\lambda u(uv)))$

Here, t and f correspond to terms representing true and false. The intended reading of a conditional $x \longrightarrow y, z$ is "if x then y, else z." The first argument in this conditional is intended to be a Boolean (t or f). Pairings ($\langle x, y \rangle$), and the projection functions on pairings (l, r) have their usual behaviour. Terms that implement these notions can in turn be defined as follows:

(150) (a) $\mathrm{t} =_{\mathrm{def}} \lambda xy(x)$
(b) $\mathrm{f} =_{\mathrm{def}} \lambda xy(y)$

(c) $x \longrightarrow y, z =_{\mathsf{def}} xyz$
(d) $\langle x, y \rangle =_{\mathsf{def}} \lambda z(zxy)$
(e) $l =_{\mathsf{def}} \lambda u(\mathrm{t})$
(f) $r =_{\mathsf{def}} \lambda u(\mathrm{f})$

As can be seen, these are defined in such a way that they have the expected behavior. It is not always simple to find a collection of terms, such as these, that implement the desired behaviour. However, when taken in isolation, the individual terms that implement a particular notion do not necessarily convey any deep intuitions about the meaning of that notion. For our purposes, all that matters is that, when taken together, the above terms implement the desired patterns of behaviour.

Addition, multiplication and the numeric equality test can be defined by way of the following equations:

(151) (a) $add(x)(y) = zero(y) \longrightarrow x, succ(add(x)(pred(y)))$
(b) $mult(x)(y) = zero(y) \longrightarrow 0, add(mult(x)(pred(y)))(x)$
(c) $x \cong_{\mathsf{Num}} y = lx \longrightarrow ly, (ly \longrightarrow lx, pred(x) \cong_{\mathsf{Num}} pred(y))$

These equations can be solved in the λ-calculus, with the expected results.

As it stands, although it indicates that Peano arithmetic is supported by any model of the untyped λ-calculus, such an implementation is not directly suited to our purposes. First, the numbers in this theory are highly extensional. Second, the test for zero relies on an extensional notion of truth, encoded by t and f.

The former presents a problem if the number theory is to be used to represent statements involving numbers that appear as arguments to proposition attitudes, for example. This is not a significant concern if the objective is merely to deal with the extensional truth conditions of cardinality statements and proportionality quantifiers.

The latter issue, concerning the extensional notions of true and false, means there is a mismatch between this implementation and our logical systems, as we do not wish to *equate* particular expressions, or terms, with truth conditions.

In the following sections we discuss proportional cardinality quantifiers, and illustrate how a number theory can be added to FIL (Chapter 4) and PTCT (Chapter 5).

6.3 Number Theory in FIL

To add Peano arithmetic to FIL, we add a new basic type N to our type system, which denotes the type of natural numbers.[37] By substituting $\cong$ for $=$ in the Peano axioms, we can formulate an intensional number theory within FIL, where 7+2 is distinguishable from 9, for example. Here we give an axiomatic presentation.

(152) $\neg\exists u_{\in N}(succ(u) \cong 0)$

(153) $\forall u, v_{\in N}(succ(u) \cong succ(v) \leftrightarrow u \cong v)$

(154) $\forall \alpha_{\in p^N}(\alpha(0) \wedge \forall u_{\in N}(\alpha(u) \rightarrow \alpha(succ(u))) \rightarrow \forall v_{\in N}\alpha(v))$

The basic arithmetical operations are defined in the usual way, but with $\cong$ substituted for $=$. In this theory it is possible for distinct representations of a number to be equivalent but not identical. Therefore, $7+2 \cong 9$, but it is not necessarily the case that $7+2 = 9$.

We can specify the relation $<$ by means of the following axiom:

(155) $\forall u, v_{\in N}(u < v \leftrightarrow \exists w_{\in N}(\neg(w \cong 0) \wedge u + w \cong v))$

6.4 Proportional Generalized Quantifiers in FIL

As mentioned above, we formulate a notion of cardinality for FIL in terms of single-place predicates, or properties. Let P be a property term in p^A, and let P^{-u} be a property term that applies to all and only the terms of which P holds except for u. We characterize the cardinality of P, $|P|$, by the following axioms:

[37] We are grateful to Tom Maibaum for suggesting this approach to the internal representation of generalized quantifiers involving cardinality relations.

(156) $\neg\exists u_{\in A} P(u) \rightarrow |P| \cong 0$

(157) $P(u) \rightarrow (\neg P^{-u}(u) \wedge \forall v_{\in A}((\neg(u \cong v) \wedge P(v)) \rightarrow P^{-u}(v)))$

(158) $P(u) \rightarrow |P| \cong |P^{-u}| + succ(0)$

The following axiom gives an interpretation of *most*, which we take to be a generalized quantifier of type $p^{(p^A)(p^A)}$:

(159) $\forall P, Q_{\in p^A}(most(P)(Q)) \leftrightarrow |\lambda u[P(u) \wedge Q(u)]| > |\lambda u[P(u) \wedge \neg Q(u)|$

6.5 Number Theory in PTCT

To add a number theory to PTCT, we need to augment the syntax and incorporate rules corresponding to the Peano axioms in Section 6.2. To the language of types, we add Num, which corresponds to the natural numbers. Numbers themselves are taken to be terms. As for the operations and tests, if an arithmetic operation results in a number, then that operation is added to the language of terms. If the operation is a test, then it is added to the language of wffs.

Closure axioms are given for the type Num and for the operations on numbers (for example, to ensure that the successor of a number is also a number), then axioms are stated that implement the Peano arithmetic itself.

As with FIL, we express the number theory in terms of extensional equivalence ($\cong$), which allows $6 + 3$ to be distinguished from $5+4$, for example, even though they have the same numeric evaluation. We could produce an extensional number theory if we replaced all relevant occurrences of $\cong$ by $=$.

(160) (a) Terms: $0 \mid succ \mid pred \mid add \mid mult \mid \hat{most} \mid |\cdot|_B$
(b) Types: Num

(c) Wffs[38]: $zero(t) \mid t \cong_{\mathsf{Num}} t' \mid t <_{\mathsf{Num}} t' \mid most(p)(q)$

The axioms for Num are the usual Peano axioms, adapted to PTCT, together with appropriate closure axioms.

(161) Closure for Num:
(a) $0 \in \mathsf{Num}$
(b) $\forall y(y \in \mathsf{Num} \rightarrow (succ(y)) \in \mathsf{Num})$

(162) Peano axioms:
(a) $\sim \exists x(x \in \mathsf{Num} \wedge succ(x) \cong_{\mathsf{Num}} 0)$
(b) $x \in \mathsf{Num} \wedge y \in \mathsf{Num} \rightarrow$
$(succ(x) \cong_{\mathsf{Num}} succ(y) \leftrightarrow x \cong_{\mathsf{Num}} y)$
(c) $zero(0)$
(d) $x \in \mathsf{Num} \rightarrow \sim zero(succ(x))$
(e) $x \in \mathsf{Num} \rightarrow pred(succ(x)) \cong_{\mathsf{Num}} x$
(f) $x \in \mathsf{Num} \rightarrow add(x)(0) \cong_{\mathsf{Num}} x$
(g) $x \in \mathsf{Num} \wedge y \in \mathsf{Num} \rightarrow$
$add(x)(succ(y)) \cong_{\mathsf{Num}} succ(add(x)(y))$
(h) $x \in \mathsf{Num} \rightarrow mult(x)(0) \cong_{\mathsf{Num}} 0$
(i) $x \in \mathsf{Num} \wedge y \in \mathsf{Num} \rightarrow$
$mult(x)(succ(y)) \cong_{\mathsf{Num}} add(mult(x)(y))(x)$
(j) $y \in \mathsf{Num} \rightarrow (0 \cong_{\mathsf{Num}} y \leftrightarrow zero(y))$
(k) $x \in \mathsf{Num} \rightarrow (x \cong_{\mathsf{Num}} 0 \leftrightarrow zero(x))$[39]

These give the basic closure axiom on 0 and its successors, the axioms corresponding to (147(a))–(147(i)), and the operations of addition, multiplication and equality, corresponding to (151(a))–(151(c)).

Here, we do not introduce an explicit term for $\perp$, and instead have axioms that are deliberately too weak to derive anything in cases where $\perp$ would otherwise arise.

We could also add the following weak induction scheme:

$$(\phi[0] \wedge \forall y(y \in \mathsf{Num} \wedge \phi[y] \rightarrow \phi[succ(y)])) \rightarrow \forall x(x \in \mathsf{Num} \rightarrow \phi[x])$$

38 We do not really need to add $t \cong_{\mathsf{Num}} t'$ to the language of wffs, as this will automatically be a wff since Num is a type, and $t \cong_T s$ is always a wff for any type T.

39 This axiom is actually redundant, given the symmetry of $\cong_T$ for all types T.

although this is not essential to our needs.

We can introduce the notion of $<_{\mathsf{Num}}$:

(163) Axioms for $<_{\mathsf{Num}}$:
(a) $y \in \mathsf{Num} \rightarrow 0 <_{\mathsf{Num}} succ(y)$
(b) $x \in \mathsf{Num} \rightarrow x \not<_{\mathsf{Num}} 0$
(c) $x \in \mathsf{Num} \wedge y \in \mathsf{Num} \rightarrow$
$(succ(x) <_{\mathsf{Num}} succ(y) \leftrightarrow x <_{\mathsf{Num}} y)$

The model theory can be extended in a straightforward way to support these new rules of the proof theory.

We can internalize the relations on natural numbers. The language of terms would then be extended with $\hat{zero}$, $\hat{<}_{\mathsf{Num}}$ corresponding to *zero*, $<_{\mathsf{Num}}$. These can be governed by the following axioms:

(164) $t \in \mathsf{Num} \rightarrow (\hat{zero}(t) \in \mathsf{Prop})$

(165) $t \in \mathsf{Num} \wedge s \in \mathsf{Num} \rightarrow (t \mathbin{\hat{<}_{\mathsf{Num}}} s) \in \mathsf{Prop}$

(166) $t \in \mathsf{Num} \rightarrow ({}^{\mathsf{T}}\hat{zero}(t) \leftrightarrow zero(t))$

(167) $t \in \mathsf{Num} \wedge s \in \mathsf{Num} \rightarrow ({}^{\mathsf{T}}(t \mathbin{\hat{<}_{\mathsf{Num}}} s) \leftrightarrow t <_{\mathsf{Num}} s)$

The treatment of typed equivalence in PTCT ensures that the notion of $\hat{\cong}_{\mathsf{Num}}$ is already present in the theory.

When we incorporate the intensional number theory into PTCT, we lose completeness of the proof theory. However, it is important to recognize that incompleteness sets in only when tableau rules that encode number-theoretic inferences are applied. The basic logic and type system of PTCT without these rules and their corresponding definitions in the model theory remains complete.

6.6 Proportional Generalized Quantifiers in PTCT

By defining the cardinality of properties, we can express the truth conditions of proportional quantifiers in PTCT.

(168) Cardinality of properties $|p|_B$:
(a) $p \in (B \Longrightarrow \mathsf{Prop}) \wedge \sim \exists x(x \in B \wedge {}^{\mathsf{T}}px) \rightarrow |p|_B \cong_{\mathsf{Num}} 0$
(b) $p \in (B \Longrightarrow \mathsf{Prop}) \wedge b \in B \wedge {}^{\mathsf{T}}pb \rightarrow$
$|p|_B \cong_{\mathsf{Num}} add(|\lambda x(px \mathbin{\hat{\wedge}} \hat{\sim}(x \mathrel{\hat{\cong}}_B b)|_B)(succ(0))$

Note that we can give an equivalent type-theoretic formulation of cardinality. This is apparent if we observe the close relationship between properties and separation types (see Sections 5.8 and 5.9).

(169) Cardinality of types $|\{x\epsilon B.px|_B$:
(a) $p \in (B \Longrightarrow \mathsf{Prop}) \wedge \sim \exists x(x \in B \wedge {}^{\mathsf{T}}px) \rightarrow$
$|\{x\epsilon B.px\}|_B \cong_{\mathsf{Num}} 0$
(b) $p \in (B \Longrightarrow \mathsf{Prop}) \wedge b \in B \wedge {}^{\mathsf{T}}pb \rightarrow$
$|\{x\epsilon B.px\}|_B \cong_{\mathsf{Num}} add(|\{x\epsilon B.px \mathbin{\hat{\wedge}} \hat{\sim}(x \mathrel{\hat{\cong}}_B b)\}|_B)(succ(0))$

We represent $most(p)(q)$ as follows:

(170) $p \in (B \Longrightarrow \mathsf{Prop}) \wedge q \in (B \Longrightarrow \mathsf{Prop}) \rightarrow$
$most(p)(q) \leftrightarrow |\{x \in B.{}^{\mathsf{T}}px \wedge \sim {}^{\mathsf{T}}qx\}|_B <_{\mathsf{Num}} |\{x \in B.{}^{\mathsf{T}}px \wedge {}^{\mathsf{T}}qx\}|_B$

Given that PTCT is a first-order theory in which all quantifi cation is first-order, this characterization of *most* effectively encodes a higher-order generalized quantifier within a first-order system.

6.7 Presburger Arithmetic

If we wish to avoid incompleteness, then we can adopt a weaker number theory, such as Presburger arithmetic (Presburger 1929). Here we give sufficient information for the interested reader to see how to adapt the treatment of numbers and cardinality given above.

The conventional presentations of Presburger arithmetic adopt the constants:

(171) $+, 1, 0, =$

together with the following axioms:

(172) (a) $\forall x \sim(0 = x + 1)$
(b) $\forall xy(\sim(x = y) \rightarrow \sim(x + 1 = y + 1))$
(c) $\forall x(x + 0 = x)$
(d) $\forall xy((x + y) + 1 = x + (y + 1))$

and the axiom schema for induction:

(173) $(\varphi[0] \wedge \forall x(\varphi[x] \rightarrow \varphi[x + 1])) \rightarrow \forall x(\varphi[x])$

Presburger arithmetic does not include multiplication, so it is not as strong as Peano arithmetic (it is not possible to formulate theorems about prime numbers, for example). However, it is adequate for the purposes of determining the truth conditions of proportional cardinality quantifiers.

Adapting these axioms to give a number theory in PTCT will result in a system that is complete, and remains semi-decidable, but which is sufficiently expressive to cope with proportional cardinality quantifiers.

6.8 Presburger Arithmetic in PTCT

Following the approach taken with Peano arithmetic, it should be clear how Presburger arithmetic can be incorporated into PTCT. First, the language has to be extended to include $+, 0, 1$ as terms. As before, the wff $t \cong_{\mathsf{Num}} s$ can serve as the notion of numerical identity. All that remains is to add closure axioms for Num and the new terms, and adapt the Presburger axioms to PTCT.

(174) Closure axioms:
(a) $0 \in \mathsf{Num}$
(b) $1 \in \mathsf{Num}$
(c) $(t \in \mathsf{Num} \wedge s \in \mathsf{Num}) \rightarrow (t + s) \in \mathsf{Num}$

(175) Presburger axioms:
(a) $x \in \mathsf{Num} \rightarrow \sim(0 \cong_{\mathsf{Num}} x + 1)$
(b) $(x \in \mathsf{Num} \wedge y \in \mathsf{Num}) \rightarrow (\sim(x \cong_{\mathsf{Num}} y) \rightarrow \sim(x + 1 \cong_{\mathsf{Num}} y + 1))$
(c) $x \in \mathsf{Num} \rightarrow (x + 0 \cong_{\mathsf{Num}} x)$
(d) $(x \in \mathsf{Num} \wedge y \in \mathsf{Num}) \rightarrow ((x + y) + 1 \cong_{\mathsf{Num}} x + (y + 1))$
(e) $(\phi[0] \wedge \forall x((x \in \mathsf{Num} \wedge \phi[x]) \rightarrow \phi[x + 1])) \rightarrow \forall x(x \in \mathsf{Num} \rightarrow \phi[x])$

Cardinality and $<_{\mathsf{Num}}$ can be treated as before.

Although Presburger arithmetic is decidable, it has some unfortunate computational properties. The time taken to decide the truth of a statement of length n is at least $2^{2^{cn}}$, for some constant c (Fischer and Rabin 1974). It may be possible to optimize the implementation of the theory in any implementation for the evaluation of the truth conditions of proportional quantifiers.

6.9 Conclusion

We have shown how number theory can be added to both FIL and PTCT. This allows us to add a notion of cardinality of properties and types, which can then be applied to state truth conditions for proportional generalized quantifiers.

Although an extensional formulation is sufficient for these purposes, we give an intensional formulation in both FIL and PTCT. This means that $6 + 3$ is intensionally distinct from $5 + 4$, for example.

In the case of PTCT, it is interesting to note that we do not need to increase the logical power of the language beyond first-order in order to be able to represent proportional generalized quantifiers. The appropriate 'sets' can be characterized within a first-order framework. However, if we adopt Peano arithmetic so as to be able to evaluate the truth conditions of such quantifiers, then the resultant theory is incomplete (following from the incompleteness of arithmetic). Fortunately, a weaker system of arithmetic, Presburger arithmetic, is sufficiently expressive to formulate the truth conditions of proportional quantifiers, and it has a decidable equality.

Given that we have numbers and cardinality in PTCT, the question arises as to whether we can express the notions of *finitely many* and *infinitely many*. To be able to do so would contradict the claim that PTCT is first-order in character. This issue is taken up in Section 9.5.

Chapter 7

Anaphora and Ellipsis

In this chapter we present a type-theoretic account of pronominal anaphora and ellipsis resolution within the framework of PTCT. We take the resolution of pronominal anaphora to be a dynamic process of identifying the value of a type parameter with an appropriate part of the representation of an antecedent. The parameter corresponds to the specification of a subtype condition on a quantified individual variable in PTCT, where the content of this condition is recovered from part of the antecedent expression. We propose a unified treatment for pronouns that accommodates bound variable, E-type, and donkey anaphora.

We represent ellipsis as the identification of a value of a separation type parameter for expressions in the ellipsis site. The separation type provides a predicate for the bare element(s) in the ellipsis structure. The value of the parameter is constructed by abstraction on an antecedent expression. When variables corresponding to pronouns are contained in the separation type retrieved from the antecedent, typing conditions on these variables are imported into the interpretation of the elided term. Different specifications of these conditions may be possible, where each specification produces a distinct reading. Using alternative resolutions of typing constraints on the pronoun variables in the ellipsis site permits us to explain the distinction between strict vs. sloppy readings of pronouns under ellipsis. It also allows us to handle antecedent contained ellipsis without invoking syntactic mechanisms such as quantifier phrase movement or semantic operations like storage. Our treatment of ellipsis is similar to the higher-order unification (HOU) analysis proposed by Dalrymple et al. (1991) and Shieber et al. (1996). However, there are a number of important differences between the two approaches which we will take up in Section 7.3.

7.1 A Type-Theoretical Approach to Anaphora

To illustrate the expressiveness of PTCT we combine our treatment of generalized quantifiers with our characterization of separation types to provide a unified type-theoretic account of anaphora.

We assume that all quantified NPs are represented as cardinality relations on the model of our treatment of *most*. Pronouns are represented as appropriately typed free variables. If the free variable is within the scope of a set forming operator that specifies a subtype and it meets the same typing constraints as the variable bound by the operator, the variable can be interpreted as bound by the operator through substitution under α identity. This interpretation yields the bound reading of the pronoun.

(176) Every man loves his mother.

(177) $|\{x \in B.{}^{\mathsf{T}}\mathsf{man}'(x) \wedge {}^{\mathsf{T}}\mathsf{love}'(x, \mathsf{mother\_of}'(y))\}|_B \cong_{Num} |\{x \in B.{}^{\mathsf{T}}\mathsf{man}'(x)\}|_B$

$\therefore$

$|\{x \in B.{}^{\mathsf{T}}\mathsf{man}'(x) \wedge {}^{\mathsf{T}}\mathsf{love}'(x, \mathsf{mother\_of}'(x))\}|_B \cong_{Num} |\{x \in B.{}^{\mathsf{T}}\mathsf{man}'(x)\}|_B$

Representations of this kind are generated by compositional semantic operations as described by (for example) Lappin (1989), and Lappin and Francez (1994).

When the pronoun is interpreted as dependent upon an NP which does not bind it, we represent the pronoun variable as constrained by a dependent type parameter whose value is supplied by context. Generally, the value of this type parameter is obtained from the predicative part of the antecedent clause representation. In the default case, the pronoun variable is bound by a universal quantifier in the language of wffs.

(178) Every student arrived.

(179) $|\{x \in B.{}^{\mathrm{T}}\mathsf{student}'(x) \wedge {}^{\mathrm{T}}\mathsf{arrived}'(x)\}|_B \cong_{Num} |\{x \in B.{}^{\mathrm{T}}\mathsf{student}'(x)\}|_B$

(180) They sang.

(181) $\forall y(y \in A \rightarrow {}^{\mathrm{T}}\mathsf{sang}'(y))$
where $A = \{x \in B.{}^{\mathrm{T}}\mathsf{student}'(x) \wedge {}^{\mathrm{T}}\mathsf{arrived}'(x)\}$

In the case of proper names and existentially quantified NP antecedents we obtain the following:

(182) John arrived.

(183) ${}^{\mathrm{T}}\mathsf{arrived}'(john')$

(184) He sang.

(185) $\forall y(y \in A \rightarrow {}^{\mathrm{T}}\mathsf{sang}'(y))$
where $A = \{x \in B.x \hat{=}_B john' \wedge {}^{\mathrm{T}}\mathsf{arrived}'(x)\}$

(186) Some man arrived.

(187) $|\{x \in B.{}^{\mathrm{T}}\mathsf{man}'(x) \wedge {}^{\mathrm{T}}\mathsf{arrived}'(x) \wedge {}^{\mathrm{T}}\varphi(x)\}|_B >_{Num} 0$

(188) He sang.

(189) $\forall y(y \in A \rightarrow {}^{\mathrm{T}}\mathsf{sang}'(y))$
where $A = \{x \in B.{}^{\mathrm{T}}\mathsf{man}'(x) \wedge {}^{\mathrm{T}}\mathsf{arrived}'(x) \wedge {}^{\mathrm{T}}\varphi(x)\}$

φ is a predicate that is specified in context and uniquely identifies a man who arrived in that context.

We handle donkey anaphora in PTCT through a type constraint on the variable corresponding to the pronoun.

(190) Every man who owns a donkey beats it.

(191) $|\{x \in B.{}^{\mathsf{T}}\mathsf{man}'(x) \wedge (|\{y \in B.{}^{\mathsf{T}}\mathsf{own}'(x,y) \wedge {}^{\mathsf{T}}\mathsf{donkey}'(y)\}|_B >_{Num} 0) \wedge \forall z(z \in A \rightarrow {}^{\mathsf{T}}\mathsf{beat}'(x,z))\}|_B$
$\cong_{Num}$
$|\{x \in B.{}^{\mathsf{T}}\mathsf{man}'(x) \wedge (|\{y \in B.{}^{\mathsf{T}}\mathsf{own}'(x,y) \wedge {}^{\mathsf{T}}\mathsf{donkey}'(y)\}|_B >_{Num} 0)\}|_B$
where $A = \{y \in B.{}^{\mathsf{T}}\mathsf{own}'(x,y) \wedge {}^{\mathsf{T}}\mathsf{donkey}'(y)\}$

The representation asserts that every man who owns at least one donkey beats all of the donkeys that he owns.

Our type-theoretic account of donkey anaphora is similar in spirit to the E-type analysis proposed by Lappin and Francez (1994). There is, however, an important difference. Lappin and Francez interpret an E-type pronoun as a choice function from the elements of an interesective set specified by the clause containing the antecedent NP to a range of values determined by this NP. Both the domain and range of the function are described informally in terms of the semantic representation of the antecedent clause. On the type-theoretic approach proposed here the interpretation of the E-type pronoun is specified explicitly through type constraints on variables in the semantic representation language. Therefore our account provides a more precise and properly formalized treatment of pronominal anaphora.

Consider the following case of donkey anaphora.

(192) Every person who had a quarter put it in a parking meter.

As Pelletier and Schubert (1989) observe, on the preferred reading of this sentence every person who had a quarter put at least one quarter that he/she had in a parking meter. We can generate these readings by treating the principle that the free variable representing a pronoun is bound by a universal quantifier as defeasible. We can then substitute an existential for a universal quantifier.

(193) $|\{x \in B.{}^{\mathsf{T}}\text{person}'(x) \wedge (|\{y \in B.{}^{\mathsf{T}}\text{had}'(x,y) \wedge {}^{\mathsf{T}}\text{quarter}'(y)\}|_B >_{Num} 0) \wedge \exists z(z \in A \wedge {}^{\mathsf{T}}\text{put\_in\_a\_parking\_meter}'(x,z))\}|_B$
$\cong_{Num}$
$|\{x \in B.{}^{\mathsf{T}}\text{person}'(x) \wedge (|\{y \in B.{}^{\mathsf{T}}\text{had}'(x,y) \wedge {}^{\mathsf{T}}\text{quarter}'(y)\}|_B >_{Num} 0)\}|_B$
where $A = \{y \in B.{}^{\mathsf{T}}\text{had}'(x,y) \wedge {}^{\mathsf{T}}\text{quarter}'(y)\}$

By taking the binding of the free variable corresponding to a pronoun by a universal quantifier as defeasible through lexical semantic and real-world knowledge factors, we are adopting a version of the pragmatic maximality condition on the interpretation of unbound pronouns proposed by Lappin and Francez (1994).

7.2 Ellipsis in PTCT

Let S be a parameter that is instantiated by separation types. We can represent a clause containing an elided VP such as (194) as (195):

(194) John sings, and Mary does too.

(195) ${}^{\mathsf{T}}\text{sings}'(john') \wedge mary' \in S$

Assuming that *mary′* and *john′* are both of type B, we can abstract on *john* to obtain the separation type $\{x \in B.{}^{\mathsf{T}}\text{sings}'(x)\}$ from the antecedent in order to resolve S. This yields the desired interpretation of the elided clause in (196).[40]

(196) ${}^{\mathsf{T}}\text{sings}'(john') \wedge {}^{\mathsf{T}}\text{sings}'(mary')$

In Section 5.9 we defined separation types to permit restricted free-floating type judgements, and so we can build up these

[40] We have omitted the assertions ${}^{\mathsf{T}}john' \epsilon B$ and ${}^{\mathsf{T}}mary' \epsilon B$ here in the interests of simplicity.

interpretations of elided expressions by compositional procedures involving the resolution of type parameters and the successive application of type membership reduction.

As we have incorporated product types into PTCT we will represent transitive and ditransitive verbs as multi-argument function terms. Our treatment of VP ellipsis extends directly to gapping (197).

(197) Mary reviewed Principia and Max Ulysses.

(198) $^{\mathsf{T}}\mathsf{reviewed}'(mary', principia') \wedge (max', ulysses') \in S$

(199) $S = \{(x, y) \in B \otimes B.{}^{\mathsf{T}}\mathsf{reviewed}'(x, y)\}$

(200) $^{\mathsf{T}}\mathsf{reviewed}'(mary', principia') \wedge {}^{\mathsf{T}}\mathsf{reviewed}'(max', ulysses')$

It also applies to pseudogapping (201).[41]

(201) Max introduced Rosa to Sam before
Bill did Mary to John.

(202) $^{\mathsf{T}}\mathsf{introduced}'(max', rosa', sam')$ before $(bill', mary', john') \in S$

(203) $S = \{(x, y, z) \in B \otimes B \otimes B.{}^{\mathsf{T}}\mathsf{introduced}'(x, y, z)\}$

(204) $^{\mathsf{T}}\mathsf{introduced}'(max', rosa', sam')$ before $^{\mathsf{T}}\mathsf{introduced}''(bill', mary', john')$

If we combine our treatment of ellipsis with our account of pronominal anaphora, the representation of the distinction between strict and sloppy readings of pronouns under ellipsis is straightforward.

(205) John loves his mother, and Bill does too.

(206) $\forall x(x \in A \rightarrow {}^{\mathsf{T}}\mathsf{loves}'(john', \mathsf{mother\_of}'(x))) \wedge bill' \in S$

[41] Here we assume, without further elaboration, that there is some suitable treatment of the temporal ordering of the circumstances described by the propositions p and q in the expression p before q.

Let S be defined as follows:

$$S = \{y \in B.\forall x(x \in A \rightarrow {}^{\mathsf{T}}\mathsf{loves}'(y, \mathsf{mother\_of}'(x)))\}$$

If the type parameter A on the variable x is specified as $\{w \in B.{}^{\mathsf{T}}w \mathrel{\hat{=}_B} john'\}$ in the antecedent clause prior to the resolution of S, then a strict reading of the pronoun results. If A is determined after the value of S is identified, then it can be taken as $\{w \in B.{}^{\mathsf{T}}w \mathrel{\hat{=}_B} bill'\}$, which provides the sloppy reading.

Finally, consider the antecedent contained ellipsis (ACE) structure in (207):

(207) Mary read every book that John did.

Restrictive relative clauses modify head nouns of NPs. Therefore, it is reasonable to impose the condition that the conjunct corresponding to a restrictive relative clause in the propositional part of the subtype expression of a GQ contains an occurrence of the variable bound by the set operator of the subtype. This is, in effect, a non-vacuousness constraint on relative clause modification. It requires that a relative clause be interpreted as a modifier that contributes a restriction to the head noun.

Given this constraint, the representation of (207) is (208):

(208) $|\{x \in B.{}^{\mathsf{T}}\mathsf{book}'(x) \wedge (john', x) \in S) \wedge {}^{\mathsf{T}}\mathsf{read}'(mary', x)\}|_B$
$\cong_{\mathsf{Num}}$
$|\{x \in B.{}^{\mathsf{T}}\mathsf{book}'(x) \wedge (john', x) \in S\}|_B$

Taking the conjunct of (208) that corresponds to the matrix clause as the antecedent and abstracting over both its arguments we obtain the separation type specified in (209). This yields (210) as the interpretation of (207).[42]

(209) $S = \{(y, w).{}^{\mathsf{T}}\mathsf{read}'(y, w)\}$

(210) $|\{x \in B.{}^{\mathsf{T}}\mathsf{book}'(x) \wedge {}^{\mathsf{T}}\mathsf{read}'(john', x) \wedge {}^{\mathsf{T}}\mathsf{read}'(mary', x)\}|_B$
$\cong_{\mathsf{Num}}$
$|\{x \in B.{}^{\mathsf{T}}\mathsf{book}'(x) \wedge {}^{\mathsf{T}}\mathsf{read}'(john', x)\}|_B$

42 For simplicity we suppress typing on the variables y and w here.

(210) asserts that every book that John read Mary read, which is the intended reading of (207).

We have generated this interpretation without using a syntactic operation of quantifier raising, as in the analysis of Fiengo and May (1994) or a semantic procedure of storage, as in the HOU treatment of Dalrymple et al. (1991). We also do not require a syntactic trace (Lappin 1996) or a SLASH feature (Lappin 1999) in the ellipsis site. The presence of the variable bound by the set operator of the subtype as the second argument of the function which assigns a value to the elided PTCT expression is motivated by a general condition on the representation of restrictive relative clauses as non-vacuous conjuncts in a GQ.

7.3 Comparison with Other Type-Theoretical Approaches

Ranta develops an analysis of anaphora within Martin-Löf Type Theory (MLTT) (Ranta 1994). He represents donkey sentences as universal quantification over product types.[43]

(211) $\Pi z : ((\Sigma x : \mathsf{man}')(\Sigma y : \mathsf{donkey}')(x\ \mathsf{owns}'\ y))$
$(p(z)\ \mathsf{beats}'\ p(q(z))$

In this example, z is a variable over product pairs, and p and q are left and right projections, respectively, on the product pair, where

(212) (a) $p(z) : \mathsf{man}'$
(b) $q(z) : (\Sigma y : \mathsf{donkey}')(p(z)\ \mathsf{owns}'\ y)$
(c) $p(q(z)) : \mathsf{donkey}'$
(d) $q(q(z)) : (p(z)\ \mathsf{owns}'\ p(q(z)))$.

There are at least two difficulties with Ranta's account. First it does not generate existential readings of donkey sentences, and

[43] Note that here expressions of the form $\Pi x : (T)(S)$ denote a dependent product type. This is not to be confused with PTCT's polymorphic types, whose form $(\Pi X.T)$ is superficially similar.

so it does not yield the prefered interpretation for sentences like (192).

Second, as Ranta acknowledges, his universal quantification-over-pairs analysis follows Discourse Representation Theory (DRT) (Kamp and Reyle 1993) in inheriting the proportion problem in a sentence like the following (Heim 1990; Kadmon 1990):

(213) Most men who own a donkey beat it.

On the universal quantification-over-pairs account of donkey anaphora, contrary to the desired interpretation, the sentence is true in a model in which ten men own donkeys, nine men own a single donkey each and do not beat it, while the tenth man owns ten donkeys and beats them all. This is because more than half the pairs of men and donkeys in this model are such that the man beats the donkey in the pair. On the preferred reading, the sentence is false in this model.

Ranta cites Sundholm's (1989) solution to the proportion problem. This suggestion involves positing a second quantifier *most* on product pairs $(\Sigma x : A)(B(x))$ that is interpreted as applying an A injection to the pairs, where this injection identifies only the first element of each pair as within the domain of quantification. Defining an additional mode of quantification as a distinct reading of *most* in order to generate the correct interpretation of (213) would seem to be an *ad hoc* approach to the difficulty. There is no evidence for taking *most* as ambiguous between two quantificational readings beyond the need to avoid the inability of the quantification-over-pairs analysis to yield the correct results for this case. Assuming two modes of quantification adds considerable complication to the type-theoretic approach to anaphora without independent motivation.

Our treatment of donkey anaphora produces existential readings for donkey sentences by allowing the free variable corresponding to a donkey pronoun to be bound by an existential rather than a universal quantifier. As we have noted, we are assuming that universal quanification of this variable is the result of a defeasible maximality condition on the interpretation of (non-bound) pronouns.

The proportion problem does not arise on our account. *Most* is represented as a cardinality relation GQ in which quantification is over the elements of the set corresponding to the subject restriction rather than over-pairs.

(214) $|\{x \in B.{}^{\mathsf{T}}\mathsf{man}'(x) \wedge (|\{y \in B.{}^{\mathsf{T}}\mathsf{own}'(x,y) \wedge {}^{\mathsf{T}}\mathsf{donkey}'(y)\}|_B >_{Num} 0) \wedge \forall z(z \in A \rightarrow \neg{}^{\mathsf{T}}\mathsf{beat}'(x,z))\}|_B$
$<_{Num}$
$|\{x \in B.{}^{\mathsf{T}}\mathsf{man}'(x) \wedge (|\{y \in B.{}^{\mathsf{T}}\mathsf{own}'(x,y) \wedge {}^{\mathsf{T}}\mathsf{donkey}'(y)\}|_B >_{Num} 0) \wedge \forall z(z \in A \rightarrow {}^{\mathsf{T}}\mathsf{beat}'(x,z))\}|_B$
where $A = \{y \in B.{}^{\mathsf{T}}\mathsf{own}'(x,y) \wedge {}^{\mathsf{T}}\mathsf{donkey}'(y)\}$

Therefore, the sentence is evaluated as false in the model that creates difficulties for DRT and for Ranta, without the need to adopt additional devices.

On the HOU approach to ellipsis proposed by Dalrymple et al. (1991) and Shieber et al. (1996), the elided predicate is represented as a higher-order variable, which is unified with a lambda term obtained from the antecedent clause through abstraction over the arguments that correspond to the bare arguments of the ellipsis site. This term is then applied to the bare arguments to produce an interpretation of the elided structure.

Our PTCT-based analysis of ellipsis is similar in approach to the HOU view. In both cases correspondences are set up between a sequence of phrases in an ellipsis site and an antecedent clause, and a predicate term is abstracted from the antecedent for application to elements in the elided clause. However, while HOU solves an equation with a higher-order variable to obtain a λ-expression, our account uses a type parameter that is resolved to a separation type expression. In our model theory, type variables take terms as values. Therefore, even if a separation type parameter is construed as a variable of PTCT, we remain within the first-order resources of PTCT.

In addition, the HOU analysis requires storage to extract a quantified NP from its antecedent-contained position in the semantic representation of an ACE structure. By contrast, we are able to interpret these NPs *in situ* by virtue of the presence of a bound variable in the part of a subtype in a GQ representation that corresponds to the relative clause of the ACE.

7.4 Conclusion

We have developed dynamic type-theoretic treatments of pronominal anaphora and ellipsis within the framework of PTCT. Our analysis of anaphora has wider empirical coverage than Ranta's (1994) MLTT analysis. Our account of ellipsis avoids the higher-order variables of HOU, and we do not require an operation of storage to handle ACE structures.

The application of PTCT to anaphora and ellipsis illustrates its considerable expressive resources. The primary advantage of PTCT is the fact that it provides the expressiveness of a higher-order system with rich typing while remaining a first-order logic with limited formal power.

Chapter 8

Underspecified Interpretations

Natural language is ambiguous with respect to the scoping of quantifiers, modifiers, conjunction, and negation. Many of these scopings are purely semantic in nature. So, for example, the following sentence allows two alternative scope readings:

(215) Every man loves a woman

(216) $\forall x(\mathsf{man}'(x) \rightarrow \exists y(\mathsf{woman}'(y) \wedge \mathsf{loves}'(x, y)))$

(217) $\exists y(\mathsf{woman}'(y) \wedge \forall x(\mathsf{man}'(x) \rightarrow \mathsf{loves}'(x, y)))$

We want our theory to produce *underspecified* representations that subsume all the various readings, and from which the different readings can be generated. We can express computable functions in PTCT, and so we can incorporate the machinery of underspecified semantics directly into the representation language.

We extend PTCT in a straightforward way to express underspecified scope representations as terms within the representation language. The expressive power of the language permits the formulation of restrictions on scope readings that cannot be captured in other theories of underspecification which rely on special purpose extra-linguistic operations and a weak system for constraint specification. We will show how in PTCT these restrictions can be encoded as filters on k-tuples of possible scope readings. Because scope representations are terms in PTCT, we can define the application of the truth predicate to these terms in a straightforward way in order to capture valid inferences in which they appear as premises. Our proof theory sustains the validity of these inferences without additional rules.

8.1 Underspecified Representations

8.1.1 Product Types as Weak Polymorphic Lists in PTCT

We have specified the type system of PTCT to include product types $S \otimes T$, which have elements of the form $\langle s, t\rangle$. Unlike monomorphic lists, the k-tuples that instantiate product types allow us to express polymorphic relations. We specify that for any k-tuple $\langle t_1, \ldots, t_k\rangle \in T_1 \otimes \ldots T_k$, the last element of the k-tuple, t_k is a designated object, like 0 or $\perp$. This condition ensures that it is possible to recognize the end of a k-tuple and thus compute its arity. The designated element of a k-tuple plays the same role as the empty list does in the tail of a list. It renders the elements of product types equivalent to weak lists with elements of (possibly) distinct types. As in the case of lists, we generally suppress this final designated element when representing a k-tuple.

8.1.2 Generalized Quantifiers as Arity Reducing Functions

In previous chapters we have interpreted Generalized Quantifiers (GQs) as corresponding to relations between the cardinalities of property terms or terms representing separation types. Here we will follow Keenan (1992) and van Eijck (2003) in generalizing this approach to one in which a GQ is taken to be an arity reduction operator that applies to a relation r to yield either a proposition or a relation r' that is produced by effectively saturating one of

r's argument with the GQ.[44] On this view, applying the GQ corresponding to *every student* to the binary relation $\lambda yx(\text{loves}'(x,y))$ gives the one-place relation $\lambda x(\text{every\_student}'(\lambda y.\text{loves}'(x,y)))$. Through β-reduction this gives $\lambda x(\forall y(\text{student}'(y) \rightarrow \text{love}'(x,y)))$, which is the property of loving every student.

On the treatment of GQs that we adopted in previous chapters, they are of type $(X \Longrightarrow \text{Prop}) \Longrightarrow \text{Prop}$, which we write Quant^X for clarity (where X is typically B). Core propositional relations, such as verbs, are of type $X_1 \Longrightarrow \ldots \Longrightarrow X_n \Longrightarrow \text{Prop}$. Slightly modifying van Eijck's (2003) Haskell-based treatment of GQs, we define an operator R to "lift" quantifiers to the appropriate level of arity reduction function on a relation.

(218) $R \in \text{Quant}^X \Longrightarrow ((X \Longrightarrow T) \Longrightarrow T)$

(219) $Q \in \text{Quant}^X \wedge r \in (X \Longrightarrow \text{Prop}) \rightarrow RQr = Qr$

(220) $Q \in \text{Quant}^X \wedge r \in (X \Longrightarrow T) \wedge (T \notin \text{Prop}) \rightarrow RQr = \lambda xRQ(rx)$

Now we can compose representations of n quantifiers with a relation r using $RQ_1(RQ_2 \ldots (RQ_n r) \ldots)$.

8.1.3 Indexed Permutations of GQ Scope Sequences

In order to construct underspecified scope representations in PTCT we need a procedure that generates the $k!$-tuple of possible scope readings that corresponds to the possible permutations of the surface sequence of GQ arguments in a core propositional relation. Following Campbell (2004), Fox and Lappin (2005) define a function that produces an indexed list of all possible

44 In Keenan's presentation, some generalized quantifiers can bind more than one of r's arguments, and so reduce its arity by more than 1. These GQs are formed from constituent quantifiers that exhibit relations of mutual dependence. Due to these relations, the GQ which they yield cannot be reduced to a simple functional composition of one quantifier with another. An example of such a GQ is ⟨*every student*, *a different book*⟩ in *Every student read a different book.*

permutations of an indexed argument list. We encoded in this function a deterministic algorithm that maps an indexed k-element list l to an indexed $k!$ list L, where each element $e_i \in L$ is the i-th permutation of l in L produced by the algorithm. We specify a function *perms_scope* that generates all $k!$ indexed permutation products of a k-ary term $\langle t_1, \ldots, t_k \rangle$ as part of the procedure for generating the set of possible scope readings of a sentence.

For our treatment of underspecification, *perms_scope* needs to take a k-ary product of scope taking elements (in the order in which they appear in the surface syntax) and a k-ary relation representing the core proposition as arguments. The scope taking elements and the core relation can be combined into a single product, e.g. as a pair consisting of the k-tuple of quantifiers as its first element and the core relation as its second. The permutation function *perms_scope* produces the $k!$-ary product of scoped readings. When a k-tuple of quantifiers is permuted, the λ-operators that bind the quantified argument positions in the core relation are permuted in the same order as the quantifiers in the k-tuple. This correspondence is necessary to preserve the connection between each GQ and its argument position in the core relation across scope permutations.

A scope reading is generated by applying the elements of the k-tuple of quantifiers in sequence to the core relation, reducing its arity with each such operation until a proposition results. The ith scope reading is identified by projecting the ith element of the indexed product of propositions that is the output by our *perms_scope* function. Below we describe a function that performs this projection of a specified scope reading. It is important to recognize that in an implementation of PTCT it is not necessary to compute the full $k!$-ary product of permutations that provides (one of the) arguments for this function until a subsequent point in the interpretation of a text or discourse. Therefore, the PTCT term consisting of the application of *perms_scope* to an input pair of a k-tuple of GQs and a core relation provides an underspecified representation of the sentence corresponding to this term. We can give a uniform type to these representations by defining arbitrary-arity product types to cover the type of the k-tuple of GQs that is the first element in the pair to which *perms_scope* applies and the $k!$-tuple which is its value.

Consider the example *Every man loves a woman*, with the GQs interpreting the subject and object NPs, the core relation, and PTCT term expressing the underspecified representation of the sentence given, respectively, as follows:[45]

(221) $Q_1 = \lambda P \hat{\forall} x \epsilon B(\mathsf{man}'(x) \hat{\rightarrow} P(x))$

(222) $Q_2 = \lambda M \hat{\exists} y \epsilon B(\mathsf{woman}'(y) \hat{\wedge} M(y))$

(223) $\lambda uv.\mathsf{loves}' uv$

(224) $perms\_scope(\langle\langle Q_1, Q_2\rangle, \lambda uv.\mathsf{loves}' uv\rangle)$

The permutations of the quantifiers relative to the core relation that we produce are

(225) $\langle\langle\langle Q_1, Q_2\rangle, \lambda uv.\mathsf{loves}' uv\rangle, \langle\langle Q_2, Q_1\rangle, \lambda vu.\mathsf{loves}' uv\rangle\rangle$

Applying relation reduction to computing the final propositions gives us a product containing the two readings.[46]

(226) $perms\_scope(\langle\langle Q_1, Q_2\rangle, \lambda uv.\mathsf{loves}' uv\rangle) =$
$\langle \hat{\forall} x \epsilon B(\mathsf{man}'(x) \hat{\rightarrow} \hat{\exists} y \epsilon B(\mathsf{woman}'(y) \hat{\wedge} \mathsf{loves}'(x, y))),$
$\hat{\exists} y \epsilon B(\mathsf{woman}'(y) \hat{\wedge} \hat{\forall} x \epsilon B(\mathsf{man}'(x) \hat{\rightarrow} \mathsf{loves}'(x, y)))\rangle$

To obtain resolved scope readings from an underspecified representation, we define a function $project\_scope^i_k$ that computes the ith permutation of a k-ary product of propositions. Specifically, it returns the i-th proposition in the product of scope readings that *perms_scope* gives as its value. We define its type as

$$\langle \mathsf{Prop}_1, \ldots, \mathsf{Prop}_k\rangle \Rightarrow \mathsf{Num} \Rightarrow \mathsf{Prop}$$

45 For ease of representation we specify GQs by traditional λ-term property encodings rather than as terms expressing cardinality relations between subtypes, as in previous chapters.

46 To simplify the exposition, the syntactic distinction between intensional term representations of propositions and extensional wffs is dropped in some of the following examples.

where $\mathsf{Num} \leq k$. To ensure that the function is total, we can define $project\_scope^i_k$ so that it projects the (i mod k)th term, for example.

8.1.4 An Alternative Perspective

Note that we can define an operation $permute^i_k$ that *directly* computes the ith permutation of a k-ary product. Given an integer i, its type will be

$$\Pi X_1 \ldots \Pi X_k(\langle X_1 \otimes \ldots X_k \rangle) \Rightarrow ((X_1 \Rightarrow \ldots X_k \Rightarrow \mathsf{Prop}) \Rightarrow \mathsf{Prop})$$

Using this approach, once we have supplied $permute^i_k$ with k quantifiers and a k-ary relation, and abstract i, the result can be taken to be an underspecified representation that denotes a (partial) function from integers to propositions. If we make the function complete, then we can define the type of these representations as

$$\mathsf{Num} \Rightarrow \mathsf{Prop}$$

As before, one way in which the function can be made complete is if $permute^i_k$ selects the (i mod k)th premutation.

8.1.5 Polymorphism in Core Relations and Generalized Quantifiers

Consider the following sentences:

(227) Every art dealer introduced a critic to two artists.

(228) Someone believes everything that Mary believes.

(229) The algorithm assigns an integer to each theorem in the logic.

In these examples *introduced* denotes a relation among three (basic) individuals, *believes* a relation between an individual and a proposition, and *assigns* a relation that holds among an abstract individual (an algorithm), a number, and a proposition. To avoid proliferating *perms_scope* functions to match each of the possible types of the core relation and its GQ arguments, it is necessary to represent these arguments as polymorphic, and to allow for a polymorphic relational type. By using product types rather than monomorphic lists as the basis for computing scope permutations we are able to do this. k-tuples can be specified for elements of distinct types.

The internal polymorphism of GQs is a somewhat more complex issue. We have been assuming that there is some way of encoding polymorphism in the type of the quantifiers representing noun phrases, so we have quantifiers with the types $(B \Longrightarrow \mathsf{Prop}) \Longrightarrow \mathsf{Prop}$ and $(\mathsf{Prop} \Longrightarrow \mathsf{Prop}) \Longrightarrow \mathsf{Prop}$, for example. Usually the type of the determiner function is fixed independently of the common noun property to which it applies. However, we could allow the type of the common noun property argument of a quantifier to determine the type of the quantifier. As it stands, this option is not directly expressible in PTCT, which adopts implicit polymorphism. In future work we will consider extending our type system to allow for explicit or parametric polymorphic typing in order to allow for this kind of type dependency. The type of a determiner would then be $(K \Longrightarrow \mathsf{Prop}) \Longrightarrow ((K \Longrightarrow \mathsf{Prop}) \Longrightarrow \mathsf{Prop})$, where K is understood as a meta-variable for some property types. The determiner's representation would require a type parameter, or constraint, that forces K to be instantiated by the same type $(A \Longrightarrow \mathsf{Prop})$ as the common noun property with which it combines.

8.1.6 Constraints on Scope Readings

There are various kinds of constraints that limit the set of possible scope readings for a particular sentence to a proper subset of the set of $k!$ orderings of the k scope taking elements which appear in it. A common condition on relative scope is the strong preference for wide scope assignment to certain quantifiers by virtue of their lexical semantic properties, like *a certain N′*.

A second kind of condition depends upon the syntactic domain in which a GQ appears. So, for example, a quantified NP within a relative clause cannot take scope over a quantified NP in which the relative clause is embedded. The following two examples illustrate these constraints.

The strongly preferred reading of (230) is the one on which *a certain book* takes wide scope relative to *every critic.*

(230) Every critic reviewed a certain book.

In (231) *every assignment* can only take narrow scope relative to *a student who completed every assignment.*

(231) A student who completed every assignment came first in the class.

Scope constraints of these kinds can be formulated as filters on the $k!$-tuple of permutations $\langle\langle Qtuple_1, Rel_1\rangle, \ldots, \langle Qtuple_{k!}, Rel_{k!}\rangle\rangle$ that *perms_scope* generates for an argument pair $\langle Qtuple_1, Rel_1\rangle$. Each such filter is a Boolean property function that imposes a condition on the elements of the $k!$-tuple.[47]

Let $\langle Quants, Rel\rangle$ be a variable ranging over pairs in which *Quants* is a k-tuple and *Rel* is a k-ary relation. We take a_certain′ to be a PTCT property that is true of all and only GQs that represent *a certain N′*, and is false of anything else. As the k-tuples are indexed, there is a one-to-one correspondence between the elements of a k-tuple and their respective indices. Let $tuple\_element(i, Quants) = Q_i$ if Q_i is a member of *Quants* and the distinguished term ω otherwise. i and j are variables ranging over integers (they are of the type Num). We can specify the lexical scope constraint illustrated in (232) as the filter in (232).

(232) $\lambda\langle Quants, Rel\rangle. \hat{\sim} (\hat{\exists} i \epsilon \mathsf{Num} \hat{\exists} j \epsilon \mathsf{Num}(\mathsf{a\_certain}'(tuple\_element(i, Quants)) \hat{\wedge} \hat{\sim} \mathsf{a\_certain}'(tuple\_element(j, Quants)) \hat{\wedge} j \hat{<}_{\mathsf{Num}} i))$

This condition requires that no element of a $k!$-tuple of scope readings contains a k-tuple of GQs in which the index of a a_certain′ GQ is higher than that of a non-a_certain′ GQ (and so outscoped by it). Notice that we have only quantified over integers (elements

[47] See van Eijck (2003) for examples of filters on lists specified as Boolean functions on the elements of a list.

of the type Num) in this filter. We have taken advantage of the isomorphism between k-tuples of integers and k-tuples of indexed GQs to avoid quantifying over GQ expressions. Therefore, we have remained within the first-order expressive resources of PTCT.

In order to formulate the condition illustrated in (231) we must introduce syntactic relations. Let relcl_embed$'(Q_1, Q_2)$ hold iff the NP corresponding to Q_2 appears in a relative clause contained in the NP corresponding to Q_1. We can formulate the constraint as in (233).

(233) $\lambda\langle Quants, Rel\rangle.$
$\hat{\sim}(\hat{\exists} i \epsilon \mathsf{Num} \hat{\exists} j \epsilon \mathsf{Num}(\mathsf{relcl\_embed}'(tuple\_element(i, Quants),$
$tuple\_element(j, Quants)) \mathbin{\hat{\wedge}} j \mathbin{\hat{<}}_{\mathsf{Num}} i))$

This filter prevents a GQ that interprets an NP in a relative clause from having scope over a GQ that interprets an NP in which the relative clause is embedded.

8.1.7 Inference with Underspecified Representations

König and Reyle (1999) propose an underspecified logic UL in which generalized rules of inference apply to underspecified representations to derive fully resolved formulas as conclusions. For example, they specify a generalized rule of *Modus Ponens* to cover inferences like (234) in which the first premise is represented by an underspecified formula that permits two scope readings.

(234) (a) Every man loves a woman.
(b) John is a man.
(c) ∴ John loves a woman.

We can capture inferences of this kind directly in PTCT by assuming that an expression of the form ${}^{\mathsf{T}}perms\_scope(\langle\langle Q_1, \ldots, Q_k\rangle, R\rangle)$ is defined as follows.

(235) ${}^{\mathsf{T}}perms\_scope(\langle\langle Q_1, \ldots, Q_k\rangle, R\rangle) =_{\mathsf{def}} {}^{\mathsf{T}}(p_1 \mathbin{\hat{\vee}} \ldots \mathbin{\hat{\vee}} p_{k!})$,
where $perms\_scope(\langle\langle Q_1, \ldots, Q_k\rangle, R\rangle) = \langle p_1, \ldots, p_{k!}\rangle$

On this definition asserting the truth of an underspecified term in PTCT asserts the truth of the disjunction of the propositional terms in the $k!$-tuple of resolved scope readings that the underspecified term returns as its value.

Van Deemter (1996) objects to a disjunctive treatment of underspecification on the following grounds. Assume that the sentence S is ambiguous between the interpretations φ and ψ, and that $\varphi \models \psi$. In this case $(\varphi \vee \psi) = \psi$, and so taking the interpretation of S to be $(\varphi \vee \psi)$ reduces S's meaning to ψ. As a result, this approach loses the distinction between a disjunction of meanings and the weakest element of the disjunction. This argument does not apply to our version of the disjunctive representation of underspecified terms in an inference. If the propositions represented by the terms $p_1 \hat{\vee} p_2$ and p_2 are such that $({}^{\mathsf{T}}p_1 \hat{\vee} p_2) \models {}^{\mathsf{T}}p_2$, then $(p_1 \hat{\vee} p_2) \cong_{\mathsf{Prop}} p_2$. But this does not imply $(p_1 \hat{\vee} p_2) =_{\mathsf{Prop}} p_2$. The two terms can be equivalent but (intensionally) distinct. Therefore we cannot substitute p_2 for $p_1 \hat{\vee} p_2$ as the representation of S. Asserting that the latter is true does not reduce to asserting that the former is true even if they represent extensionally equivalent propositions. Van Deemter's criticism of the disjunctive treatment of underpecified premises in an inference turns on an extensional interpretation of the disjunction and its elements. Because we take the relevant premises to assert the truth predicate of intensional representations of propositions, and PTCT distinguishes between provable equivalence (in a type T) and intensional identity (in T), we avoid this criticism.[48]

The inference in (234) is represented as (236):

(236) (a) ${}^{\mathsf{T}}(\hat{\forall} x \epsilon B(\mathsf{man}'(x) \hat{\rightarrow} \hat{\exists} y \epsilon B(\mathsf{woman}'(y) \hat{\wedge} \mathsf{loves}'(x,y)))$
$\quad\hat{\vee}\ \hat{\exists} y \epsilon B(\mathsf{woman}'(y) \hat{\wedge} \hat{\forall} x \epsilon B(\mathsf{man}'(x) \hat{\rightarrow} \mathsf{loves}'(x,y))))$

(b) ${}^{\mathsf{T}}\mathsf{man}'(john')$

(c) $\therefore\ {}^{\mathsf{T}}\hat{\exists} y \epsilon B(\mathsf{woman}'(y) \hat{\wedge} \mathsf{loves}'(john', y)))$

The tableau rules that we presented in Chapter 5 sustain this inference.

48 We are grateful to Christian Ebert for pointing out van Deemter's argument to us, and for helpful discussion of the argument.

We could follow König and Reyle (1999) in formulating generalized inference rules that apply to classes of terms to yield conclusions that follow from the disjunctions corresponding to these terms by the tableau rules given in Chapter 5. This device would permit us to use the assertion of truth for a *perms_scope* term as a premise in an inference without computing the $k!$-tuple of scoped propositions that is the value of the function for its arguments in the term. However, it is important to observe that such generalized rules are a purely abbreviational device for representing classes of inferences supported by the proof theory of PTCT. They do not add additional rules or formal power to this proof theory.

8.2 Comparison with Other Theories

8.2.1 Storage

Cooper (1983) and Pereira (1990) define a procedure of quantifier storage. In the course of computing the compositional interpretation of a clause, the rules of semantic derivation apply storage to a quantified NP by substituting a variable for the GQ interpretation of the NP and adding the GQ to the storage set. A GQ is stored as the first element of a pair whose second element is the variable that is left in its argument position. The representation produced for the clause consists of the core propositional relation and a set of stored GQ pairs. When a GQ is discharged from storage, it is applied to the core relation, binding the variable in its original position. As the elements of the storage set are unordered, they can be discharged in any sequence, where each sequence yields a possible scope reading. So, for example, when storage is applied to the subject and object GQs in (237), the resulting representation (using a version of Pereira's (1990) notation) is (238):

(237) Most students read two articles.

(238) $\{\langle \mathsf{most\_students}', x\rangle, \langle \mathsf{two\_articles}', y\rangle\} \vdash \mathsf{read}'(x, y)$

The two possible orders for discharging the quantifiers from storage give the scope readings in (239) and (240):

(239) most_students′(λx(two_articles′(λy(read′(x, y))))))

(240) two_articles′(λy(most_students′(λx(read′(x, y))))))

Storage provides an elegant and straightforward way of generating underspecified scope representations for a sentence. However, there are (at least) three difficulties with this approach. First, storage is an additional mechanism defined outside of the semantic representation language as such. The expressions that it produces are not themselves part of this language (a typed λ-calculus) but stages in the derivation of well-formed terms of the representation language. While storage is easily implemented in a declarative fashion, as in Pereira (1990) and Blackburn and Bos (2005), it remains an essentially procedural device that is added to a compositional semantic theory as a means of obtaining scope ambiguity without attaching alternative scope readings to distinct syntactic structures, as in Montague (1974).

By contrast, in our account, underspecified representations are themselves terms of PTCT, the representation language. Therefore, this issue does not arise.

Second, as the storage set is unordered, it is not obvious how to project a particular scope reading without computing all $k!$ readings from the set. This problem is partially solved when storage is actually implemented, as the storage set becomes an ordered list. However, in order to allow for the projection of a specified scope reading without constructing all permutations of a list l, it is necessary to develop additional procedures for representing the $k!$ list L of l's permutations, and projecting the i-th element of L without actually computing all the elements of L. While this is possible, these procedures have to be defined as additional mechanisms outside of the representation language (say, a typed λ-calculus).

This problem does not arise on our approach. Underspecified representations consist in the application of a scope permutation function to an indexed k-tuple, which yields a term of PTCT. The $k!$-tuple that is the value of the function at an argument need not be fully computed to project a specified scope reading. A projection function can compute the product up to the i-th element and then stop, returning the i-th value. Product types, permutation functions on k-tuples, and projection functions on indexed k-tuples are all defined within the resources of PTCT.

Finally, because storage is a mechanism constructed outside of the representation language, it is necessary to specify an additional constraint language for stating the Boolean conditions required to restrict the set of possible scope readings derived from the storage set.[49]

Again, this problem does not arise on our treatment of underspecification. The filters that express constraints on scope readings are λ-terms of PTCT, and so the resources required for the formulation of these constraints are available within the representation language.

8.2.2 Holes, Plugs, and Glue Languages

Bos (1995) and Blackburn and Bos (2005) develop a constraint-based system for underspecified representation for first-order logic that they refer to as *Predicate Logic Unplugged* (PLU). This system is a generalization of the *hole semantics* approach to underspecification which Reyle (1993) first developed within the framework of Underspecified Discourse Representation Theory. Copestake *et al.*'s (1997) Minimal Recursion Semantics is an adaptation of hole semantics within a typed-feature structure grammar (HPSG).

An underspecified representation of a quantified first-order formula in PLU is an ordered tripe $\langle LH, F, R \rangle$. LH is a set of labels for formulas and of holes, which are metavariables that take formulas as values. F is a set of labelled formulas, which may

49 Keller (1988) defines a type of storage that encodes relations of syntactic nesting within the stored GQ corresponding to an NP that contains another quantified NP. Although these nested stores avoid certain problems of variable binding encountered with Cooper storage, they do not, in themselves, impose constraints on possible scope readings of the sort that we have discussed in the previous section. See Blackburn and Bos (2005) for a discussion and an implementation of Keller stores.

contain holes for subformulas. R is a set of scope constraints expressed as partial order relations on labels and holes. The PLU representation of (241) is (242):

(241) Every student wrote a program.

(242) $\langle\{l_1, l_2, l_3, h_0, h_1, h_2\},$
$\{l_1 : \forall x(\text{student}'(x) \rightarrow h_1), l_2 : \exists y(\text{program}'(y) \wedge h_2),$
$l_3 : \text{wrote}'(x, y)\},$
$\{l_1 \leq h_0, l_2 \leq h_0, l_3 \leq h_1, l_3 \leq h_2\}\rangle$

The partial ordering constraints in (242) define a bounded lattice with h_0 as $\top$, the propositional core of the formula, l_3 as $\perp$, and l_1 and l_2 as midpoints of the lattice between $\top$ and $\perp$. As l_1 and l_2 are not ordered with respect to each other, either formula can be substituted for the hole in the other formula. l_3 must be substituted last in the remaining hole. If l_1 is taken as the value of h_0, l_2 is substituted for h_1, and then l_3 is substituted for h_2, the result is a wide scope reading of the universal quantifier, as in (243). Alternatively, if l_2 is taken as the value of h_0, l_1 is assigned to h_2, and l_3 to h_1, we obtain (244):

(243) $\forall x(\text{student}'(x) \rightarrow \exists y(\text{program}'(y) \wedge \text{wrote}'(x, y)))$

(244) $\exists y(\text{program}'(y) \wedge \forall x(\text{student}'(x) \rightarrow \text{wrote}'(x, y)))$

These are the only two scope resolutions that satisfy the partial order conditions in (242).

Hole semantics provides a more expressive and flexible system for constructing underspecified representations than storage. It generalizes naturally to scope elements other than GQs, like negation and modifiers. It is possible to identify a particular scope reading that satisfies the constraints of an underspecified hole semantic representation by imposing a particular order of substitution of labels for holes in a schematic formula set. However, it does suffer from the first and third difficulties which we raised against storage. Underspecified representations are constructed out of metavariables, schematic formulas, and partial ordering statements in a metalanguage that is distinct from the semantic representation language. The substitutions of labelled formulas for holes that generate the well-formed formulas of the representation language which correspond to scope readings are also metalinguistic operations added to the representation language.

More seriously Ebert (2003) shows that PLU and other hole semantic systems are expressively incomplete because their constraint languages do not permit the formulation of Boolean conditions on scope such as those formulated in (232) and (233). As in the case of storage, it is possible to add a constraint language with sufficient expressive power required to state conditions of this kind.[50] But this requires a further enrichment and complication of the theory. As we have seen, the problems do not arise on our account.

Dalrymple et al. (1999) and Crouch and van Genabith (1999) suggest a theory on which representations of GQs and core relations are expressed as premises in an underspecified semantic glue language. These premises are combined by the natural deduction rules of linear logic in order to yield a formula that represents the scope reading of a sentence. The rules can apply to premises in different orders of derivation to generate alternative scope readings. Unlike PLU the glue language can be higher-order. The formal properties of glue language semantics are different than hole semantics, but it is closely related to this approach in the general view of underspecification that it adopts. It would seem that in order achieve expressive completeness in the sense of Ebert (2003), glue language semantics must add a system for stating constraints on the linear logic proof theory which it employs to derive specified interpretations.

8.3 Conclusion

We have presented a treatment of underspecified representation within PTCT which uses product types rather than lists to

50 We are grateful to Ian Pratt-Hartmann for helpful discussion of this point.

represent scope sequences. These types permit us to accommodate polymorphism in the core relation arguments.

We have characterized an underspecified representation as a PTCT term in which a function *perms_scope* applies to a pair containing an initial sequence of scope taking elements and a core relation. It returns as its value an indexed $k!$-product of possible scope readings. $project\_scope(perms\_scope(\langle Qs, Rel\rangle), i)$ projects the i-th scope reading in the $k!$-tuple of scope readings $perms\_scope(\langle Qs, Rel\rangle)$.

We have formulated constraints on scope readings as filters on the $k!$-tuples that *perms_scope* produces. These filters are PTCT property terms which encode Boolean conditions and quantification over the integers of indexed k-tuples.

We have defined the application of the truth predicate to *perms_scope* terms in a way that permits us to accommodate valid inferences involving underspecified premises directly within PTCT, where these inferences follow from our proof theory without the addition of new rules.

Underspecified representations, the projection of a particular scope reading, constraints on possible scope readings, and inferences with underspecified premises are all expressed by appropriately typed λ-terms within the semantic representation language, PTCT, rather than through operations on schematic metalinguistic objects.

Chapter 9

Expressive Power and Formal Strength

In this chapter, some of the arguments for and against the use of higher-order logics for natural language semantics are discussed. We claim that first-order logics can be made sufficiently expressive to deal with most key issues in natural language semantic, and that given a choice between a higher-order theory and a first-order theory, the latter is to be preferred. We also discuss some other issues that are relevant to theories, like PTCT, which are sufficiently expressive to be able to internalize their own type system.

9.1 Decidability and Completeness

A decidable theory is one in which it is possible to compute all the theorems and non-theorems. Recursively enumerable theories allow us to compute all the theorems, but not necessarily all the non-theorems. They can be described as 'semi-decidable'.

In general, theories that are not recursively enumerable will not be complete with respect to their models. There will be valid sentences for which proofs cannot be found. However, for some models the set of valid sentences may lie within the set of theorems that *are* recursively enumerable. In other words, there will be classes of models with respect to which the logic is complete (Henkin 1950). If the phenomena that we are formalizing falls within this class of models, then the proof theory will be complete, and all the appropriate theorems will be recursively enumerable.

When considering a particular theory, there are two general concerns: whether the theory is *expressive* enough to represent salient issues conveniently, and whether it is *powerful* enough for us to perform appropriate inferences. If we are concerned about being able to perform effective reasoning, then we might wish to avoid theories that are so powerful that their theorems are not recursively enumerable. Under this criterion, a first-order system is preferable to a higher-order system, if it is sufficiently expressive for the relevant domain.

Unfortunately, in the case of natural language semantics, basic first-order logic by itself does not provide the features that are required. It is insufficiently expressive for our purposes. This gives rise to a source of tension here, as one way of increasing a theory's expressiveness is to increase its power. For example, the ability to express properties of sets and relationships between them can be achieved by moving to a higher-order theory. Some would argue that it is indeed 'natural' to do so, despite the fact that the theorems of such systems are not recursively enumerable.

However, if we are concerned about issues of formal power, and related computational issues, then we should reconsider whether we need the full force of higher-order logic. For example we might not need to express properties and relationships over all sets, only some of them. If this is the case, then we do not need the full force of a higher-order theory (Henkin 1950), and we can produce systems tailored to the problem at hand, whose theorems are recursively enumerable.

In the case of the two main theories presented in this book, FIL adopts the higher-order approach, whereas PTCT is specifically given a weaker formulation, where we can express properties and relationships that seem appropriate for natural language semantics, without making an overt commitment to the power of a higher-order system.

9.2 Arguments for Higher-Order Theories

Although rarely spelt out in detail, there are some standard arguments in favour of adopting higher-order theories for natural language semantics. Basic first-order logic appears inadequate for any general theory of natural language semantics because it is insufficiently expressive. For example, there is no notion of modality, of intensionality, or of type. All these are required for a viable semantic theory. These concerns can be addressed by adopting a more powerful theory.

Theories such as Montague's IL (Montague 1974) (Section 1.1) avoid the weaknesses of first-order logic by providing a treatment of types, modality, intensionality, time, and (with some tweaks), anaphoric issues (Groenendijk and Stokhof 1990, 1991). Arguably, the higher-order regime arises 'naturally' if we seek to achieve formal simplicity and uniformity in the presentation of the logic. It is perhaps for this reason that higher-order systems have dominated the field in natural language semantics despite the fact that the set of theorems of such systems is not recursively enumerable.

Given compositionality of the models for IL, and the compositional translation of natural language into IL, it is even possible to eliminate the logic as a level of representation, and just consider the interpretation of natural language in set theory. As set theory provides a foundation for mathematics, this means (in principle at least), that any notion which can be expressed mathematically can be captured. The full resources of mathematics can be brought to bear on any semantic problem, provided a suitable 'encoding' can be found.

Following this approach, there is no issue that lies beyond formalization. Further, it could be argued that the set theory underlying the models of IL has an independently motivated existence, and that this justifies its use in natural language semantics.

Finally, it can also be argued that we are obliged to adopt a powerful theory if we wish to incorporate arithmetic, which is required for proportional cardinality quantifiers. Indeed, if we add arithmetic to a logic, regardless of whether it is first-order or higher-order, the theorems will not be recursively enumerable. This result is independent of whether or not we express cardinality quantifiers by way of quantification over sets.

9.3 Arguments against Higher-Order Theories

If we are interested in building practical natural language systems, then it is appropriate to worry about the computational properties of a semantic theory. In general, powerful logics, such as IL and other higher-order logics are not recursively enumerable. That is, we cannot find proofs of all theorems. This is an unpleasant property of these systems. Even so, one might claim that this is not sufficient motivation for avoiding powerful theories. It could be that the issue of incompleteness can be avoided in most cases of practical concern through computational devices such as imposed upper bounds on the maximal length of a formula (or a sentence). However, there are other arguments against the view that higher-order logic is appropriate *because* it is so powerful and 'natural.'

The arguments concerning the acceptability, or appropriateness of powerful theories given above are not applied in other aspects of natural language analysis. Few people (if anyone) would suggest that the most powerful theory should be adopted for syntax (e.g. a Turing equivalent notation) just because it *is* the most powerful theory, and hence can express any grammatical relationships that we might ever wish to represent. From the perspective of scientific methodology, one attempt to identify the *weakest* theory that can account for the data (or at least, the one with the fewest 'bells and whistles'), as such theories will provide the greater explanatory power with the fewest assumptions.

Furthermore, finding an encoding of a phenomenon in some general purpose theory, such as set theory, that happens to give the appropriate results does not necessarily mean that we have understood the true nature of the issue, or captured it in terms that provide any genuine insight. As an example, consider the encoding of Peano arithmetic in λ-calculus given in Section 6.2.

We might wonder how representing 0 by $\lambda x.x$ provides any insight into its role in number theory. Similarly with set theory, encoding 0 as the empty set may confuse as much as it helps. The empty set can be used as the denotation of other notions, such as the collection of even prime numbers. The encoding into set-theory may simply conflate ideas that are actually distinct.

It may be hard to find a good encodings of a particular problem. If it does not incorporate certain properties of the relevant phenomena, the underlying theory that the encoding invokes can make it difficult to capture a concept accurately. One is then tempted to settle for an inferior solution, merely because it is easier to express. In effect, the decision to adopt some powerful, general purpose theory may impose unmotivated constraints on the analysis. The treatment of intensionality in IL may be one such case.

As an alternative to adopting a higher-order theory, we can take a weaker system and increase its expressivity by adding types (or features that resemble them), intensionality, and modality. The question then arises as to how much of this machinery we can import into a relatively simple logic without creating a system that, even without the addition of Peano arithmetic, is as powerful as IL, or set theory. The arguments for and against higher-order logic can then be characterized as a choice between either adopting a pre-existing logic, or building a logic that is tailored to the problem in hand.

Number theory presents a problem. As already noted, when we add number theory to a logic, we have a powerful system that is not recursively enumerable. One way out of this problem is to adopt a weaker system of arithmetic that appears adequate for the purposes at hand, such as Presburger arithmetic (Section 6.7). Even with Peano arithmetic, the problems of incompleteness arise only when reasoning with statements that include arithmetic expressions.

PT, a first-order Property Theory (Section 3.4) (Aczel 1980; Turner 1992), goes a long way towards obtaining an appropriately expressive theory that remains first-order. It shows that there are viable first-order theories for natural language semantics.

9.4 Self-Application, Stratification and Impredicativity

A serious problem with PT is that it does not allow the notion of proposition (or truth) to be internalized or to be used in intensional contexts (Section 3.4.5). But there are cases where it may be appropriate to use an intensional analogue prop′ of the predicate Prop, which characterizes propositions. For example, it seems natural to constrain the domain of quantification in the following sentence so that the bound variables range only over propositions:

(245) John believes everything Mary believes.

If this sentence itself appears in an intensional context, then we need an intensional analogue prop′ of Prop to appear as part of an intensional term:

(246) $\hat{\forall} x((\mathsf{prop}'(x) \mathbin{\hat{\wedge}} \mathsf{bel}'(mary')(x)) \mathbin{\hat{\rightarrow}} \mathsf{bel}'(john')(x))$

But as we saw in Section 3.4.5, if we add the term representation prop′ of the PT predicate Prop (or term representation for the PT predicate True which characterizes truth), then the theory becomes inconsistent. This inconsistency would arise through a variant of Russell's paradox.

To avoid inconsistency, we could try to use the term $\mathfrak{prop}$, the weak internalization of Prop (see (97), page 52), in place of prop′.

(247) $\hat{\forall} x((\mathfrak{prop}(x) \mathbin{\hat{\wedge}} \mathsf{bel}'(mary')(x)) \mathbin{\hat{\rightarrow}} \mathsf{bel}'(john')(x))$

Unfortunately, because of the unbounded quantification we cannot prove that the representation of the sentence as given in (247) is a proposition, and so we cannot consider its truth conditions.

For these reason, in PT any restrictions on the domain of quantification in the representation of quantified propositions have to be imposed externally (Turner 1990, 1997).

In contrast, PTCT does allow us to express constraints of this kind on the domain of quantification quite naturally, because the type of propositions can appear in intensional contexts.

The paradoxes are avoided because PTCT does not allow self-application. The alternative to this restriction would be to impose appropriate constraints on the domain of quantification within the meta-language.

An interesting consequence follows from the fact that the PTCT type Prop can be used to constrain the domain of quantification in intensional representations of propositions. The notion of proposition in PTCT is impredicative. To see this, consider the term $\hat{\forall} x \epsilon \mathsf{Prop}(s)$. This will be a proposition if $s[x/t]$ is a proposition for all propositions t. That is

$$\forall x(x \in \mathsf{Prop} \rightarrow s \in \mathsf{Prop}) \rightarrow \hat{\forall} x \epsilon \mathsf{Prop}(s) \in \mathsf{Prop}$$

However, these propositions include $\hat{\forall} x \epsilon \mathsf{Prop}(s)$, iff it is a proposition. For this reason, the set of propositions cannot be characterized within PTCT. This may appear paradoxical, but it is not. In this case it would only be paradoxical if we sought to define the set of propositions within the theory, or if the theory supported self-application.

If we wish both to allow self-application, and represent examples such as (245) using an internal notion of proposition, then the impredicative nature of propositions cannot be sustained. Instead, as previously discussed (Section 3.4.6), a stratified theory would have to be adopted, where we posit a hierarchy of languages, each of which internalizes the notion of proposition for the language below it in the hierarchy (Turner 2004). This alternative deserves serious consideration, but we do not adopt it here.

9.5 First-Order Status and Finite Cardinality

We claim that PTCT is a first-order system. This requires some clarification. Although the syntax of the wffs in PTCT is expressed as a first-order language, in itself the syntactic form of a theory is not a reliable guide to its formal power. Even powerful theories such as set theory and higher-order logic can be stated in the form of a first-order *theory*; that is, as a first-order *logic* with additional axioms. We wish to claim that PTCT is not merely a syntactically first-order theory, but that it is formally weaker in its expressive power than second-order logic.

When considering whether or not a theory is genuinely first-order or not, it is useful to consider what can be expressed within that theory. There are certain formal notions that cannot be expressed within a first-order framework, such as *finitude*, *well-ordered* and *well-founded* (Eklund 1996). If we can properly express such notions within PTCT, then PTCT has (at least) the expressive resources of a second-order theory.

Let us examine the notion of *finitude*. A typical second-order definition of this notion is as follows:

(248) $$FINITE(P) =_{\mathrm{def}} \sim \exists f[\ \forall xy(fx = fy \rightarrow x = y) \wedge \forall x(P(x) \rightarrow P(fx)) \wedge \exists y(P(y) \wedge \forall x(P(x) \rightarrow fx \neq y))]$$

This definition states that there is no bijection f on P which maps elements of P to a proper subset of P. It is the negation of the usual statement of infinitude. Expressed in PTCT, in the case where $P \in (B \Longrightarrow \mathsf{Prop})$, this becomes:

(249) $$FINITE_B(P) =_{\mathrm{def}} P \in (B \Longrightarrow \mathsf{Prop}) \wedge \sim \exists f[\forall xy((x, y \in B \wedge fx =_B fy) \rightarrow x =_B y) \wedge \forall x((x \in B \wedge {}^{\mathsf{T}}P(x)) \rightarrow {}^{\mathsf{T}}P(fx)) \wedge \exists y(y \in B \wedge {}^{\mathsf{T}}P(y) \wedge \forall x((x \in B \wedge {}^{\mathsf{T}}P(x)) \rightarrow fx \neq_B y))]$$

If this properly expresses the property of 'having finite cardinality,' then it can be shown that PTCT is not first-order (for example, see Eklund (1996, footnote 8)).

How, then, do we avoid this problematic conclusion? First, we observe that in first-order Property Theory (PT, Section 3.4), finitude of a property P can also be encoded schematically by:

(250) $$FINITE^{\mathsf{PT}}(P) =_{\mathrm{def}} \mathsf{Pty}(P) \wedge \sim \exists f[\forall xy(fx = fy \rightarrow x = y) \wedge \forall x(\mathsf{True}(P(x)) \rightarrow \mathsf{True}(P(fx))) \wedge \exists y(\mathsf{True}(P(y)) \wedge \forall x(\mathsf{True}(P(x)) \rightarrow fx \neq y))]$$

This suggests that if PTCT is not first-order, then neither is 'first-order' Property Theory.

To see why these definitions do not undermine the claim to first-order status for PTCT (and PT), observe that the existentially quantified variable f ranges over representations of *computable* functions, rather than all functions.[51] The definitions given are not then *proper* definitions of finitude. The function f is intended to be a bijection in P. In the case of PTCT and PT, any attempt to formalize the notion of P having finite or infinite extension is restricted to the consideration of *computable* bijections. This is because, in both cases, the terms of the logic are those of the untyped λ-calculus, which are interpreted as representing computable functions.

If our claim is correct, and these definitions of finitude are not *proper*, then there will be sets that cannot be classified correctly. In particular, our definitions should be incomplete, and any model for finitude, for example, need not exclude certain infinite sets. This should also be true of any alternative characterizations of (in)finite, such as the (non)existence of a bijection from the set to the set of numbers.

As an example, let A be a set that is infinite, enumerable, and non-well-ordered. Unlike Num and other well-ordered sets, it does not have an initial element corresponding to 0. We assume that there is a bijective mapping from A to Num. However, we cannot, in general, effectively compute for any bijective mapping $f : A \Longrightarrow A$, a y such that for any x it is or is not the case that $f(x) = y$. So we cannot identify A as either finite or as infinite in models of PTCT according to the standard definition of a finite set that we have given. Therefore, PTCT cannot express *(in)finitely many* as a general property of sets.

A possible reply to this argument is to note that the bijection $g : A \Longrightarrow$ Num is sufficient to show that A is infinite, as Num can be shown to be infinite by a computable bijection, such as $+n$. However, g is not, itself, a demonstrably computable function.

51 The computable functions are recursively enumerable as they can be generated from the syntax of the λ-calculus.

We are simply assuming it for the argument, and it cannot be invoked to show that A is infinite.

As we have defined cardinality in PTCT (Chapter 6), it appears then that we could also define finitude as follows:

(251) $\mathit{finite} =_{\mathsf{def}} \lambda p(\hat{\exists} n \epsilon \mathsf{Num}(|p|_B \hat{=}_{\mathsf{Num}} n))$

This will form a proposition with terms of type $B \Longrightarrow \mathsf{Prop}$. Note, however, that in Chapter 6 we defined $|\cdot|_B$ in the language of wffs, not the language of terms. So (251) requires a change to the language of wffs. For the present purposes, we can work around this issue by giving a schematic definition.

(252) $\mathit{finite}'(X) =_{\mathsf{def}} \exists n(n \in \mathsf{Num} \wedge |X|_B =_{\mathsf{Num}} n)$

Again, the question arises as to whether this properly captures a notion of finitude. Although the notion does capture all finite sets, the definition is not effectively decidable with infinite sets.[52]

In summary, we cannot capture proper notions of (in)finitude in PTCT (or PT), although we can express a weaker notion, which we might term *first-order definable (in)finitude*. This gives us reason to believe that PTCT, like PT, is essentially first-order in its formal power. However, in order to substantiate the claim that PTCT is a first-order logic (as opposed to merely a first-order *theory*), we need to demonstrate that PTCT is conservative with respect to a *bona fide* first-order logic.

We can strengthen and generalize our claim concerning the first-order status of PTCT by considering Henkin's (1950) result for second-order logic. Second-order logic is incomplete relative to the standard model, in which the subset relation and the domain of functions (sets) is fixed. Henkin shows that second-order logic is complete for the class of general models (general function spaces), which includes non-standard models that do not respect the fixed specifications of the standard model.

Enderton (2001) presents Henkin's result in an elegant way by first demonstrating that any first-order many-sorted theory L_m

52 Our definition of $|X|_B$ also assumes some means of recursing through the set (i.e. that there is some form of choice function).

has a countable model. Enderton then proves that a second-order theory can be translated into an equivalent first-order many-sorted theory (a first-order many-sorted theory is in turn reducible to a first-order one-sorted theory). Given such a translation, the second-order theory is interpreted by the set of general models, and so it is complete.

When interpreted by general models, second-order logic effectively becomes a first-order theory in its expressive power. Consider the following statement:

(253) Any bounded, non-empty, well-ordered set has a least upper bound.

When (253) is expressed in a second-order theory that is interpreted by the standard model, it applies to the power set of the set of natural numbers, which has the cardinality of the set of real numbers. Therefore, second-order logic with the standard model gives us a statement that is true of the set of real numbers. However, there are non-standard models in which all sets are countable, and relative to these models (253) does not identify the set of real numbers.

It might be suggested that PTCT is a second-order theory which achieves first-order expressive power by using a model theory that generates something similar to the set of general models. While this idea has a core of truth, it does not quite capture the source of the constraint on PTCT's formal power. In our model theory the terms correspond to computable functions, of which there are countably many. As all properties and sets which can be described by sentences of PTCT are term representable, they are also countable. It follows that in every model in which the PTCT representation of (253) holds, it will only be true of properties corresponding to countable sets.[53] As all models are countable in the model theory for PTCT, it is constrained to first-order expressive power.

[53] A similar argument has been made for PT. Fox (2000) shows that a statement equivalent to (253) can be stated in first-order PT because the quantification over sets can only range over PT definable sets.

9.6 Relevance of PTCT to Computational Semantics

The question is then whether it would be more appropriate to formulate a logic that directly incorporates the constraints of the phenomena under consideration. This is the objective of PTCT, to produce a recursively enumerable logic by encoding sufficient expressive power for natural language semantics within a first-order framework. In its language of terms, PTCT encodes the expressive aspects of a higher-order system. The power of the system is restricted by constraints on these encodings. In PTCT, quantification ranges only over terms, and all notions used in our semantic theory are term representable. The constraints on the terms ensure that they are genuinely first-order in character.

As we have observed, although adding Peano arithmetic increases the formal power of a logic and leads to a theory that is no longer recursively enumerable, it is possible to use weaker theories of arithmetic (Section 6.7), which are adequate for proportional cardinality quantifiers. Further, in the representation of such quantifiers, we can use first-order term representations of 'sets.' So such quantifiers in themselves do not require that we adopt more powerful theories, provided that we satisfy the constraints we have imposed on the term representability of types, properties, and propositions.[54]

We believe that the features of PTCT make it particularly appropriate for implementing theorem proving systems for natural language semantics. It adds significant 'expressiveness' to a first-order theory, without an undesirable increase in formal power.

9.7 Conclusion

PTCT is a first-order system whose expressiveness is designed for natural language semantics. Unlike Montague's IL, it directly

[54] Clearly there are some outstanding issues if we wish to reason with statements about mathematics or computer programs.

supports fine-grained intensionality and a flexible system of types. We have formulated tableau rules for PTCT, which provide an effective first-order theorem proving procedure for the underlying logic and type system of the theory. Unlike higher-order logic (and IL in particular), the proof theory is complete. There are other choices that could have been made in formulating the theory, such as adopting a stratified type system, which would then allow certain cases of self-application. These merit further attention.

Chapter 10

Conclusion

In this monograph we have taken up a number central issues in the formal foundations of semantic theory. We will summarize our conclusions by revisiting the main points of our study.

10.1 Montague Semantics and the Architecture of Semantic Theory

We started with a discussion of the architecture of Montague semantics, focusing on its view of intensions, its type theory, and the power of the logic within which it develops a theory of meaning. Montague's characterization of intensions as functions from possible worlds to denotations, inherited from Carnap (1947), has dominated formal semantics for the past sixty years. It forces the reduction of intensional identity to extensional equivalence across the set of worlds, and renders the notion of intension dependent upon modal concepts. The result is an empirically inadequate rough-grained view of meaning that remains an unsolved problem for many current semantic theories.

Montague's higher-order type theory, adapted from Church's (1940) STT, provides IL with significant expressive power, but it is not sufficiently flexible or articulated to capture important properties of natural language intepretation. The meanings for many natural language expressions exhibit polymophism. In addition, separation and product types play an important role in the representation of anaphora and ellipsis. In order to achieve a type system that includes these elements, it is necessary to move beyond Church typing.

Finally, while classical first-order systems do not have sufficient expressive resources to provide a semantic representation language for natural language, the fact that IL is a higher-order logic raises serious questions of excessive formal and computational power. If a higher-order representation language is not constrained, then the set of its provable theorems is not recursively enumerable.

While most post-MS theories have constructed task-specific systems to deal with particular limitations of MS we have sought to address these three foundational problems. Therefore we have highlighted general questions of formal design in the construction of a semantic theory.

10.2 Algebraic Semantics and Fine-Grained Alternatives to MS

We found it useful to formulate a generic possible worlds semantics of the IL variety in algebraic terms in order to clarify the task of constructing a fine-grained intensional theory. We used this algebraic model as a paradigm against which to evaluate several post-MS hyperintensionalist systems.

Two options for a formally viable fine-grained intensional logic emerged from this investigation. One involves extending the set of worlds (situations) to include cases in which the axioms governing the non-logical constants of the theory are violated. This is the impossible worlds strategy, which is implicit in the proposals of Barwise and Perry (1983) and Muskens (1995). It retains the Carnap–Montague view of intensions as functions from worlds (situations) to denotations. It distinguishes between expressions that share denotations across possible worlds by expanding the set of worlds to include those that do not satisfy the constraints that specify the intended interpretations of the language. These can be thought of as non-standard models of the semantic theory.

Barwise (1997) suggests an epistemic interpretation of impossible worlds as expressions of the range of possibilities allowed by a state of partial knowledge. As one's knowledge increases, this range is progressively narrowed and impossible worlds are eliminated. Despite its elegance, this view has the unfortunate consequence of rendering the theory of meaning entirely dependent upon an account of belief and cognition. Specifically, it excludes the possibility of recognizing as distinct in meaning two expressions that one knows to be extensionally equivalent in all possible situations. In order to sustain this possibility, it is necessary to specify intensions independently of denotations and of cognitive state.

The other option involves taking intensions to be basic elements of one's model theory which cannot be reduced to functions from indices to denotations. This strategy requires representing the set of propositions in one's theory as a bounded prelattice in which a non-antisymmetric preorder models the entailment relation. Within such a prelattice, provably equivalent propositions are not necessarily identical, and so we avoid intensional collapse of the kind that undermines IL. This approach is implicit in Bealer (1982), and we proposed it in earlier work (Fox and Lappin 2001, 2003; Fox et al. 2002a, 2002b, 2002c). We adopt this view as the basis for our treatment of intensions.

10.3 A Conservative Revision of MS

Initially we restricted ourselves to implementing the second strategy for achieving fine-grained intensionality while holding the other main features of MS constant. This produced FIL, a higher-order system with Church typing in which we dispense with the axiom of extensionality and introduce distinct equality predicates for intensional identity and extensional equivalence. These predicates allow us to express the difference between equivalence and intensional identity within the representation language.

The semantics for FIL is specified in terms of a bounded semi-lattice of propositions with a non-antisymmetric preorder. Intensions of appropriate types are assigned to the non-logical constants of the language, and possible worlds are defined as ultra filters of the prelattice of propositions. The truth-value of a proposition at a world w is determined by its membership or non-membership in w. The denotation of an individual constant is an equivalence class of individual intensions at w, and the denotation corresponding to a functional type B^A is a function from intensions of type A to denotations at w of type B. Therefore, we invert the Carnap–Montague approach to intensionality by defining denotations in terms of intensions. Modal operators are quantifiers over worlds, and so modality, like denotations, is constructed on the basis of intensional entities, specifically ultrafilters of propositions.

Although FIL solves the problem of fine-grained intensionality without recourse to impossible worlds, it leaves the difficulties emanating from the type system and the higher-order logic of IL untouched.

10.4 Enriching Property Theory with Curry Typing

We have seen that untyped Property Theory (Chierchia and Turner 1988; Turner 1987, 1992) effectively implements the second strategy for fine-grained intensionality within an extended first-order language. It contains the untyped λ-calculus as a language of terms that represent intensional entities, like propositions. A first-order language of well-formed formulas that includes a truth predicate and a predicate which holds of propositional terms is used to specify the truth conditions of propositions. Distinct terms can denote propositions that are provably equivalent, and so intensional collapse is avoided. Semantic paradoxes are blocked by limiting the truth predicate to propositional terms and ruling out problematic definability relations between certain predicates in the language of wffs and corresponding property terms.

As PT is first-order, it is possible to achieve recursive enumerability of its theorems. However, it lacks a type system, and so it is limited in expressive resources. Types can be simulated through the introduction of sorts in the domain. However, this still does not allow for genuine polymorphism. Moreover, the predicate characterizing propositions is not internally definable as a property within the term language.

We introduce Curry typing into PT to obtain PTCT. This gives us a first-order representation language that provides fine-grained intensionality, limited formal power, and a richly expressive type system. We incorporate the equality predicates for intensional identity and extensional equivalence, respectively, into both the language of terms and the language of wffs. The use of Prop as a type allows us to control the application of the truth predicate in wffs. We also place constraints on the propositional terms that can appear in the specification of separation and comprehension types. Specifically, we limit free-floating type judgements in these contexts. These restrictions filter out semantic paradoxes.

We specify a tableau proof theory and a model theory for PTCT, and we prove the soundness and completeness of the proof procedure relative to the model theory.

PTCT is, then, a semantic representation language that solves the three foundational problems with IL that we sought to address.

10.5 An Intensional Number Theory

Many semantic theories assume the existence of natural numbers without formally introducing them. We define a type Num for both FIL and PTCT, and we add an intensional number theory to each language. We then give a recursive definition of the cardinality of properties in FIL, and of property terms and separation types in PTCT. These definitions supply the basis for a treatment of generalized quantifiers as relations between the cardinality of properties and, in PTCT, of separation types. In the case of PTCT we encode higher-order GQs like *most* as terms in a first-order language.

Because we use versions of the Peano axioms for our intensional number theories, we import the full power of arithmetic into FIL and PTCT. Consequently, we lose the completeness of PTCT when we extend its type system to include Num. One way of avoiding this result is to use a weaker number theory, such as Presburger arithmetic, which contains addition but not multiplication. Such a system is sufficient to support our recursive definition of cardinality for property terms and separation types. While Presburger arithmetic restores completeness, it does so at the cost of prohibitive complexity. In future work we will look at possible bounding constraints on this and other treatments of numbers in order to achieve both completeness and computational tractability for that part of number theory which we require for natural language semantics.

10.6 A Dynamic Type-Theoretic Account of Anaphora and Ellipsis

We apply PTCT to anaphora and ellipsis resolution to construct a dynamic type theoretic account of these phenomena. Pronouns are represented as variables with associated type parameters. The value of such parameters is a separation type computed from the representation of a generalized quantifier antecedent. By using a defeasible pragmatic maximality condition to determine the kind of quantifier that binds the pronominal variable, we generate both universal and existential readings of donkey sentences. On our account the GQ which provides the antecedent for a donkey pronoun quantifies over a property rather than pairs of objects. Therefore, we avoid the proportion problem that undermines the classical DRT analysis and Ranta's MLTT-based treatment of relative clause donkey sentences.

We use product separation types to extend our type-theoretic view of anaphora to ellipsis. On our approach, resolving ellipsis consists in the identification of a value of a separation type parameter for expressions in the ellipsis site. The separation type provides a predicate for the bare element(s) in the ellipsis structure. The value of the parameter is constructed by abstraction on an antecedent expression.

When variables corresponding to pronouns are contained in the separation type retrieved from the antecedent, typing conditions on these variables are imported into the interpretation of the elided term. Different specifications of these conditions may be possible, where each specification produces a distinct reading. Using alternative resolutions of typing constraints on the pronoun variables in the ellipsis site permits us to explain the distinction between strict vs sloppy readings of pronouns under ellipsis. It also allows us to handle antecedent contained ellipsis without invoking syntactic mechanisms such as quantifier phrase movement or semantic operations like storage. Our treatment of ellipsis is similar to the higher-order unification analysis proposed by Dalrymple et al. (1991) and Shieber et al. (1996). However, unlike HOU we do not use higher-order property variables but first-order type parameters that take terms as values.

10.7 Underspecified Interpretations as λ-Terms of the Representation Language

Using product types we construct λ-terms within PTCT to express underspecified scope relations. These terms consist of a function *perms_scope* applied to a pair consisting of a k-tuple Qs of scope taking elements and a relational term Rel, corresponding to the main verb of a sentence, where Rel takes the members of Qs as its arguments. The value of the function for a pair $\langle Qs, Rel\rangle$ is the indexed $k!$-product of possible scope readings that result from the $k!$ permutations of Qs. Constraints on possible scope readings are formulated as filters on this function, where each filter is also a λ-term.

We use the term $project\_scope_k{}^i(perms\_scope(\langle Qs, Rel\rangle))$ to identify the ith scope reading of the $k!$-ary product of possible scope readings that $perms\_scope(\langle Qs, Rel\rangle)$ produces. In general, it is not necessary to compute the full $k!$ product to obtain this scope reading. Moreover, computation of a *perms_scope* term can be delayed until filters are extracted from subsequent discourse to restrict the search space of possible scope readings.

Given our definition of the application of the truth predicate to λ-terms expressing underspecified scope readings, the proof theory that we specify for PTCT covers valid inferences involving propositions with underspecified scope interpretations in the premises. Generalized inference rules can be formulated to apply directly to the λ-terms, but these would be purely abbreviational devices that identify classes of independently valid inference patterns. They would not add new rules or formal power to the proof theory.

Unlike other current theories of underspecified interpretation, our account generates underspecified representations within the object language rather than within a metalanguage. We do not require additional operations on object language expressions, nor do we posit a new constraint language. Underspecified representations and filters on the functions that provide them are terms of PTCT, and so they are available as part of the expressive resources of the representation language. PTCT yields an account of underspecified interpretation without requiring any formal enrichment of the theory.

10.8 PTCT and Computational Semantics: Directions for Future Work

The next phase in our research on the foundations of semantic theory will focus on implementing PTCT as a framework for natural language interpretation. In focusing on the properties of an adequate semantic representation language we have set aside issues concerning the syntax–semantics interface. We will address these issues by integrating PTCT into a grammar-parser. In principle, PTCT should be compatible with any computational grammar in which the semantic interpretation of a phrase is computed in parallel with its syntactic structure. However, there is an obvious formal commensurability between PTCT and Categorial Grammar (CG), given that both theories are versions of the λ-calculus. We will examine different formulations of CG to see which one is best suited to the incorporation of PTCT as the module of semantic interpretation.

In addition to using PTCT to construct the semantic component of a grammar-parser, we intend to implement our type-theoretic treatments of anaphora and ellipsis resolution. We will also experiment with the generation of underspecified scope representations. This will involve investigating the use of constraints that are incrementally acquired in parsing and discourse interpretation to determine the selection of a particular scope reading from the initial set of possible interpretations that an underspecified representation makes available.

Finally, we will attempt to implement the tableau proof theory for PTCT as a theorem prover. We hope to be able to show that this system will provide an efficient procedure for testing and identifying relations of semantic implication, equivalence, and intensional identity.

Our main concern in writing this monograph has been to return to a number of formal problems in semantic theory that, for the most part, have been relegated to the margins of the field for many years. We are convinced that these are central issues that cannot be passed over if semantic theory is to rest on solid foundations. If our work provokes even modest discussion of the questions that we raise in this book, then we will have succeeded in our aim.

Bibliography

Aczel, P. (1980). Frege structures and the notions of proposition, truth and set. In Barwise, J., Keisler, J., and Keenan, E., editors, *The Kleene Symposium*, North Holland Studies in Logic, pp. 31–9. North Holland.

Barendregt, H. (1984). *The Lambda Calculus: Its Syntax and Semantics*, volume 103 of *Studies in Logic and the Foundation of Mathematics*. North Holland, Amsterdam, second edition.

Barwise, J. (1997). Information and impossibilities. *The Notre Dame Journal of Formal Logic*, 38: 488–515.

Barwise, J. and Cooper, R. (1981). Generalised quantifiers and natural language. *Linguistics and Philosophy*, 4: 159–219.

Barwise, J. and Etchemendy, J. (1990). Information, infons, and inference. In Cooper, R., Mukai, K., and Perry, J., editors, *Situation Theory and Its Applications*, volume 1, pp. 33–78. CSLI, Stanford, CA.

Barwise, J. and Perry, J. (1983). *Situations and Attitudes*. MIT Press (Bradford Books), Cambridge, MA.

Bealer, G. (1982). *Quality and Concept*. Clarendon Press, Oxford.

Bell, J. (1999). Boolean algebras and distributive lattices treated constructively. *Mathematical Logic Quarterly*, 45, 135–43.

Benthem, J. van (1991). *Language in Action*. Studies in Logic. North-Holland, Amsterdam.

Beth, E. W. (1956). L'existence en mathématiques. In *Collection de logique mathématiques, série A*. Gauthier-Villars/Naewelaerts, Paris, Louvain. (Beth's lectures at the Sorbonne University (Paris), March 29–April 2, 1954.)

Blackburn, P. and Bos, J. (2005). *Representation and Inference for Natural Language*. CSLI, Stanford, CA.

Bos, J. (1995). Predicate logic unplugged. In *Proceedings of the Tenth Amsterdam Colloquium*. Amsterdam, Holland.

Campbell, W. H. (2004). Indexing permutations. *Journal of Computing in Small Colleges*, 19: 296–300.

Carnap, R. (1947). *Meaning and Necessity*. University of Chicago Press, Chicago.

Chierchia, G. (1982). Nominalisation and Montague grammar: a semantics without types for natural languages. *Linguistics and Philosophy*, 5: 303–54.

Chierchia, G. (1984). *Topics in the Semantics of Infinitives and Gerunds*. PhD thesis, University of Massachusetts, Amherst. Published in 1989 by Garland, New York.

Chierchia, G. (1995). *Dynamics of Meaning*. University of Chicago Press, Chicago.

Chierchia, G. and Turner, R. (1988). Semantics and property theory. *Linguistics and Philosophy*, 11: 261–302.

Church, A. (1940). A formulation of the simple theory of types. *Journal of Symbolic Logic*, 5: 56–68.

Cocchiarella, N. B. (1979). The theory of homogeneous simple types as a second order logic. *Notre Dame Journal of Formal Logic*, 20: 505–24.

Cooper, R. (1983). *Quantification and Syntactic Theory*. Synthese Language Library. D. Reidel, Dordrecht.

Cooper, R. (1996). The role of situations in generalized quantifiers. In Lappin, S., editor, *The Handbook of Contemporary Semantic Theory*, pp. 65–86. Blackwell, Oxford.

Copestake, A., Flickinger, D., and Sag, I. A. (1997). Minimal recursion semantics. Technical report, Stanford University, Stanford, CA, unpublished ms.

Cresswell, M. J. (1985). *Stuctured Meanings*. MIT Press, Cambridge, MA.

Crouch, D. and van Genabith, J. (1999). Context change, underspecification, and the structure of glue language derivations. In Dalrymple, M., editor, *Semantics and Syntax in Lexical Functional Grammar*, pp. 117–89. MIT Press, Cambridge, MA.

Dalrymple, M., Lamping, J., Pereira, F., and Saraswat, V. (1999). Quantification, anaphora, and intensionality. In Dalrymple, M., editor, *Semantics and Syntax in Lexical Functional Grammar*, pp. 39–89. MIT Press, Cambridge, MA.

Dalrymple, M., Shieber, S., and Pereira, F. (1991). Ellipsis and higher-order unification. *Linguistics and Philosophy*, 14: 399–452.

Dávila-Pérez, R. (1994). Constructive type theory and natural language. Computer Science Memorandum 206, University of Essex.

Dávila-Pérez, R. (1995). Semantics and parsing in intuitionistic categorial grammar. PhD thesis, University of Essex.

Deemter, K. van (1996). Towards a logic of ambiguous expressions. In van Deemter, K. and Peters, S., editors, *Semantic Ambiguity and Underspecification*, pp. 203–37. CSLI, Stanford, CA.

Dowty, D., Wall, R., and Peters, S. (1981). *Introduction to Montague Semantics*. D. Reidel, Dordrecht.

Ebert, C. (2003). The expressive completeness of underspecified representations. In *Proceedings of the Fourteenth Amsterdam Colloquium*. Amsterdam, Holland.

Eijck, J. van (2003). Computational semantics and type theory. unpublished ms., CWI, Amsterdam.

Eklund, M. (1996). On how logic became first-order. *Nordic Journal of Philosophical Logic*, 1(2): 147–67.

Enderton, H. B. (2001). *A Mathematical Approach to Logic*. Academic Press, New York.

Fiengo, R. and May, R. (1994). *Indices and Identity*. MIT Press, Cambridge, MA.

Fischer, M. J. and Rabin, M. O. (1974). Super-exponential complexity of Presburger arithmetic. In *Proceedings of the SIAM-AMS Symposium in Applied Mathematics*, volume 7, pp. 27–41.

Fitting, M. (1996). *First-Order Logic and Automated Theorem Proving*. Springer-Verlag, Berlin.

Fitting, M. (2000). Higher-order modal logic—A sketch. In Caffera, R. and Salzar, G., editors, *Automated Deduction in Clasical and Non-Classical Logics*, Springer Lecture Notes in Artificial Intelligence, pp. 23–38. Springer-Verlag, Berlin and New York.

Fitting, M. and Mendelsohn, R. (1999). *First-Order Modal Logic*. Kluwer, Dordrecht.

Fox, C. (2000). *The Ontology of Language*. CSLI Lecture Notes. CSLI, Stanford, CA.

Fox, C. and Lappin, S. (2001). A framework for the hyperintensional semantics of natural language with two implementations. In de Groote, P., Morrill, G., and Retore, C., editors, *Logical Aspects of Computational Linguistics*, Springer Lecture Notes in Artificial Intelligence, pp. 175–92. Springer-Verlag, Berlin and New York.

Fox, C. and Lappin, S. (2003). Doing natural language semantics in an expressive first-order logic with flexible typing. In Jaeger, G., Monachesi, P., Penn, G., and Wintner, S., editors, *Proceedings of Formal Grammar 2003*, pp. 89–102. Technical University of Vienna, Vienna.

Fox, C. and Lappin, S. (2005). Underspecified interpretations in a Curry-typed representation language. *Journal of Logic and Computation*, 15: 129–41.

Fox, C., Lappin, S., and Pollard, C. (2002a). First-order Curry-typed logic for natural language semantics. In Winter, S., editor, *Proceedings of the 7th International Workshop on Natural Language Understanding and Logic Programming*, pp. 175–92, Copenhagen, University of Copenhagen.

Fox, C., Lappin, S., and Pollard, C. (2002b). A higher-order fine-grained logic for intensional semantics. In Alberti, G., Balough, K., and Dekker, P., editors, *Proceedings of the Seventh Symposium for Logic and Language*, pp. 37–46, Pecs, Hungary, University of Pecs.

Fox, C., Lappin, S., and Pollard, C. (2002c). Intensional first-order logic with types. In Alberti, G., Balough, K., and Dekker, P., editors, *Proceedings of the Seventh Symposium for Logic and Language*, pp. 47–56, Pecs, Hungary, University of Pecs.

Frege, G. (1892). On sense and reference. In Geach, P. and Black, M., editors, *Translations from the Philosophical Writings of Gottlob Frege*, 3rd Edition, pp. 56–78. Basil Blackwell, Oxford.

Gallin, D. (1975). *Intensional and Higher-Order Modal Logic*. North-Holland, Amsterdam.

Gazdar, G. (1980). A cross-categorial semantics for coordination. *Linguistics and Philosophy*, 3: 407–9.

Gilmore, P. C. (2001). An intensional type theory: Motivation and cut-elimination. *Journal of Symbolic Logic*, 66: 383–400.

Gregory, H. (2002). Relevance logic and natural language semantics. In *Proceedings of Formal Grammar 2002*, Trento, Italy.

Groenendijk, J. and Stokhof, M. (1990). Dynamic Montague grammar. In Kálmán, L. and Polós, L., editors, *Papers from the Second Symposium on Logic and Language*, pp. 3–48, Budapest, Hungary, Akadémiai Kiadó. Also available as ITLI Prepublication Series LP–90–02.

Groenendijk, J. and Stokhof, M. (1991). Dynamic predicate logic. *Linguistics and Philosophy*, 14(1): 39–100.

Heim, I. (1982). The semantics of definite and indefinite noun phrases. PhD thesis, University of Massachusetts, Amherst. Thesis distributed by Graduate Linguistics Student Association.

Heim, I. (1990). E-type pronouns and donkey anaphora. *Linguistics and Philosophy*, 13: 137–77.

Henkin, L. (1950). Completeness in the theory of types. *Journal of Symbolic Logic*, 15: 323–44.

Jeffrey, R. (1982). *Formal Logic: Its Scope and Limits*. McGraw-Hill, New York.

Johnstone, P. T. (1982). *Stone Spaces*. Cambridge University Press, Cambridge.

Jonsson, B. and Tarski, A. (1951). Boolean algebras with operators. *American Journal of Mathematics*, 73: 891–939.

Kadmon, N. (1990). Uniqueness. *Linguistics and Philosophy*, 13: 237–324.

Kamareddine, F. (1995). Important issues in foundational formalisms. *Bulletin of the Interest Group in Pure and Applied Logics*, 3(2,3): 291–317.

Kamp, H. (1981). Theory of truth and semantic representation. In Groenendijk, J. A. K., Janssen, T. M. V., and Stokhof, M. B. J., editors, *Formal Methods in the Study of Language*, Mathematical Centre Tracts 135, pp. 277–322. Amsterdam.

Kamp, H. and Reyle, U. (1993). *From Discourse to Logic: Introduction to Modeltheoretic Semantics of Natural Language, Formal Logic and Discourse Representation Theory*. Kluwer, Dordrecht.

Keenan, E. (1992). Beyond the Fregean boundary. *Linguistics and Philosophy*, 15: 199–221.

Keenan, E. and Stavi, K. (1986). A semantic characterization of natural language determiners. *Linguistics and Philosophy*, 9: 253–326.

Keenan, E. and Westerståhl, D. (1997). Generalized quantifiers in linguistics and logic. In van Benthem, J. and ter Meulen, A., editors, *Handbook of Logic and Language*, pp. 838–93. Elsevier, Amsterdam.

Keller, W. (1988). Nested Cooper storage: The proper treatment of quantification in ordinary noun phrases. In Reyle, U. and Rohrer, C., editors, *Natural Language Parsing and Linguistic Theories*. Reidel, Dordrecht.

König, E. and Reyle, U. (1999). A general reasoning scheme for underspecified representations. In Ohlbach, H. J. and Reyle, U., editors, *Logic, Language, and Reasoning: Essays in Honour of Dov Gabbay*. Kluwer, Dordrecht.

Kripke, S. (1959). A completeness theorem in modal logic. *Journal of Symbolic Logic*, 24: 1–14.

Lambek, J. and Scott, P. (1986). *An Introduction to Higher Order Categorial Logic*. Cambridge University Press, Cambridge.

Landman, F. (1986a). Data semantics: An epistemic theory of partial objects. In *Towards a Theory of Information: The Status of Partial Objects in Semantics*, Groningen-Amsterdam Studies in Semantics, pp. 1–96. Foris, Dordrecht.

Landman, F. (1986b). Pegs and alecs. In *Towards a Theory of Information: The Status of Partial Objects in Semantics*, Groningen-Amsterdam Studies in Semantics, pp. 97–136. Foris, Dordrecht.

Lappin, S. (1989). Donkey pronouns unbound. *Theoretical Linguistics*, 15: 263–86.

Lappin, S. (1996). The interpretation of ellipsis. In Lappin, S., editor, *The Handbook of Contemporary Semantic Theory*, pp. 145–75. Blackwell, Oxford.

Lappin, S. (1999). An HPSG account of antecedent contained ellipsis. In Lappin, S. and Benmamoun, E., editors, *Fragments: Studies in Ellipsis and Gapping*, pp. 68–97. Oxford University Press, New York.

Lappin, S. (2000a). An intensional parametric semantics for vague quantifiers. *Linguistics and Philosophy*, 23: 599–620.

Lappin, S. (2000b). An introduction to formal semantics. In Aronoff, M. and Rees-Miller, J., editors, *The Blackwell Handbook of Linguistics*, pp. 369–93. Blackwell, Oxford.

Lappin, S. (2003). Semantics. In Mitkov, R., editor, *The Handbook of Computational Linguistics*, pp. 91–111. Oxford University Press, Oxford.

Lappin, S. and Francez, N. (1994). E-type pronouns, I-sums, and donkey anaphora. *Linguistics and Philosophy*, 17: 391–428.

Lappin, S. and Pollard, C. (1999). A hyperintensional theory of natural language interpretation without indices or situations. MS., King's College, London and Ohio State University.

Larson, R. and Segal, G. (1995). *Knowledge of Meaning*. MIT Press, Cambridge, MA.

Maibaum, T. (1997). Conservative extensions, interpretations between theories and all that! In Bidoit, M. and Dauchet, M. M., editors, *TAPSOFT '97: Theory and Practice of Software Development*, pp. 40–66, Springer-Verlag, Berlin and New York.

Martin-Löf, P. (1982). Constructive mathematics and computer programming. In Cohen, L. J., Los, J., Pfeiffer, H., and Podewski, K.P., editors, *Logic, Methodology and Philosophy of Science VI*, pp. 153–79. North Holland.

Martin-Löf, P. (1984). *Studies in Proof Theory (Lecture Notes)*. Bibliopolis, Napoli.

McCord, M. and Bernth, A. (forthcoming). A metalogical theory of natural language semantics. *Linguistics and Philosophy*.

Meyer, A. (1982). What is a model of the lambda calculus? *Information and Control*, 52: 87–122.

Montague, R. (1974). *Formal Philosophy: Selected Papers of Richard Montague*. Edited with an introduction by R. H. Thomason. Yale University Press, New Haven, CT/London.

Muskens, R. (1995). *Meaning and Partiality*. CSLI and FOLLI, Stanford, CA.

Naur, P. (1960). Revised report on the algorithmic language ALGOL 60. *Communications of the ACM*, 3(5): 299–314.

Partee, B., ter Meulen, A., and Wall, R. (1990). *Mathematical Methods in Linguistics*. Kluwer, Dordrecht.

Pelletier, J. and Schubert, L. (1989). Generically speaking. In Chierchia, G., Partee, B. H., and Turner, R., editors, *Properties, Types, and Meaning*, volume 2, pp. 193–267. Kluwer, Dordrecht.

Pereira, F. (1990). Categorial semantics and scoping. *Computational Linguistics*, 16: 1–10.

Pollard, C. (2004). Type-logical HPSG. In Jäger, G., Monachesi, P., Penn, G., and Wintner, S., editors, *Proceedings of the Ninth Annual Conference on Formal Grammar 2004*, pp. 107–24, Nancy.

Presburger, M. (1929). Über die Vollständigkeit eines gewissen Systems der Arithmetik ganzer Zahlen, in welchem die Addition als einzige Operation hervortritt. In *Comptes Rendus du I Congrès de Mathématiciens des Pays Slaves, Warszawa*, pp. 92–101.

Quine, W. V. O. (1960). *Word and Object*. MIT Press, Cambridge, MA.

Ranta, A. (1991). Intuitionistic categorial grammar. *Linguistics and Philosophy*, 14: 203–39.

Ranta, A. (1994). *Type Theoretic Grammar*. Oxford University Press, Oxford.

Reyle, U. (1993). Dealing with ambiguities by underspecification: Construction, representation and deduction. *Journal of Semantics*, 10: 123–79.

Sag, I. A. (2003). Coordination and underspecification. In Kim, J.-B. and Wechsler, S., editors, *Proceedings of the Ninth International Conference on HPSG*, pp. 267–91, Stanford, CA.

Seligman, J. and Moss, L. (1997). Situation theory. In van Benthem, J. and ter Meulen, A., editors, *Handbook of Logic and Language*, pp. 239–309. Elsevier, North Holland, Amsterdam.

Shieber, S., Pereira, F., and Dalrymple, M. (1996). Interactions of scope and ellipsis. *Linguistics and Philosophy*, 19: 527–52.

Smith, J. M. (1984). An interpretation of Martin-Löf's Type Theory in a type-free theory of propositions. *Journal of Symbolic Logic*, 49: 730–53.

Smullyan, R. M. (1968). *First-Order Logic*. Springer-Verlag, Berlin.

Sundholm, G. (1989). Constructive generalised quantifiers. *Synthese*, 79: 1–12.

Thomason, R. (1980). A model theory for propositional attitudes. *Linguistics and Philosophy*, 4: 47–70.

Turner, R. (1987). A theory of properties. *Journal of Symbolic Logic*, 52(2): 455–72.

Turner, R. (1988). Properties, propositions, and semantic theory. In *Proceedings of Formal Semantics and Computational Linguistics*, Switzerland.

Turner, R. (1990). *Truth and Modality for Knowledge Representation*. Pitman, London.

Turner, R. (1992). Properties, propositions and semantic theory. In Rosner, M. and Johnson, R., editors, *Computational Linguistics and Formal Semantics*, Studies in Natural Language Processing, pp. 159–80. Cambridge University Press, Cambridge.

Turner, R. (1997). Types. In van Benthem, J. and ter Meulen, A., editors, *Handbook of Logic and Language*, pp. 535–86. Elsevier, North Holland, Amsterdam.

Turner, R. (2005). Semantics and stratification. *Journal of Logic and Computation*, 15(2).

Zalta, E. N. (1988). *Intensional Logic and the Metaphysics of Intensionality*. MIT Press/Bradford Books, Cambridge, MA.

Author Index

Subject Index